living with art

THIS IS A CARLTON BOOK

Design copyright © 2000 Carlton Books Limited
Text copyright © 2000 Karen Wheeler
This edition was published by Carlton Books Limited in 2000
20 Mortimer Street
London W1N 7RD

A CIP catalogue for this book is available from the British Library

ISBN 1 84222 068 3

Editorial Manager: Venetia Penfold
Art Director: Penny Stock
Project Editor: Zia Mattocks
Copy Editor: Sarah Sears
Designer: Maggi Smith
Picture Editor: Abi Dillon
Production Controller: Janette Davis

Printed and bound in Dubai

living with art

Karen Wheeler

CARLTON
BOOKS

contents

YES, BUT IS IT ART?

Art. To many people the word itself is intimidating. It suggests priceless Rembrandts, unattainable paintings in museums and antique objects you cannot afford. The headline-grabbing sums of money for which Old Master paintings change hands at auction only serve to reinforce this impression. Many people think that they only encounter art in museums, and that there is little likelihood of ever being able to display a work of art at home.

In fact, we are all surrounded by images and objects in our homes which perform aesthetic as well as functional roles. Art not only describes pretty pictures that cost the earth but also all kinds of decorative objects which exist in a domestic setting, including carpets, textiles, ceramics and furniture. There are myriad opportunities to introduce art into the home: the way a child's painting is pinned to a fridge door; the way you arrange pictures or furniture in a room; even the colour of wall paint is a form of artistic expression.

Art is becoming more accessible and does not need to be expensive. Original paintings are still the most desirable, but photographs, posters, limited-edition prints and lithographs – all of which can be bought for the price of dinner in a decent restaurant – may also be considered 'works of art' and are more available to people than ever before. Habitat, for example, now sells limited-edition prints by Turner-prize finalists, proving that the quest for individual art has reached the street and a larger part of the population.

At the same time the definition of art is constantly evolving. Experimentation in other media fields, like video and sound installations, has pushed back boundaries. Damien Hirst's shark in formaldehyde or Tracey Emin's embroidered tent and unmade bed are not intended for a domestic environment but they have helped to stretch the definition of art. Emin, for example, prints, draws, makes appliqué blankets, videos and sculptural constructions. Her childish scrawls on pieces of paper tacked to a wall, her personal letters or the pages she has torn from newspapers and pasted into frames, are as far removed from a polite Victorian watercolour as you can get; yet before their relocation to

London's Tate Modern they hung in the Tate Gallery under the same roof as nineteenth-century painters such as J M W Turner.

Emin's work proves the point that art is in the eye of the beholder. An object that one person considers ugly or mundane can be a thing of exquisite beauty to another. Jean Cocteau once said, 'Art produces ugly things which frequently become beautiful with time.' We owe a lot to the Pop Art era of the 1950s and 1960s for knocking elitist art off its pedestal, for although Pop artists were derided by many of their contemporaries, they took inspiration from domestic culture and everyday objects such as soup cans and Coco-Cola bottles and paved the way for the acceptance of more unusual forms of art today.

the art of interiors

A wall without a picture is like a rose without scent and suggests a place that is unlived in. Whether your living space is a single small room or a massive open-plan loft, a picture is often the magical factor that turns four walls and a ceiling into a home, stamped with your style. Indeed, artists, fashion designers and photographers use their homes as striking reflections of their own creativity.

The burgeoning interest in art for the home is also part of the increasingly image-led world of contemporary interior design. Interiors today not only continually blur the barriers between fine and applied art, they also demonstrate that the gap between art and decor is becoming increasingly vague. There remains, however, one crucial difference between the two: over time, art usually becomes more meaningful and you grow emotionally more attached to it.

Owning an expensive painting is a status symbol for some people, which is why multi-million-pound Van Gogh's so often end up in the executive offices of big banks. As Thomas Hoving, former director of the Metropolitan Museum of Art in New York once declared: 'Art is sexy! Art is money-sexy. Art is money-sexy-social-climbing fantastic!' There is, indeed, something deeply sexy about owning, say, a Picasso. For most of us, however, buying a painting or a poster is more about stylish interior design, rather than climbing the ladder of respectability. It is about creating an environment that expresses your taste and individuality. Nevertheless, whether you favour brooding portraits or friendly folk art, your choice in paintings does act as an important social indicator. The person who favours bold Pop Art posters or black-and-white prints by Robert Mapplethorpe, for example, is likely

LEFT: ART IN THE CONTEMPORARY HOME CAN COME IN MANY GUISES – FROM FURNITURE AND CANVASES TO FUNKY INSTALLATIONS.

'You use a glass mirror to look at your face: you use works of art to see your soul.'

George Bernard Shaw.

to have a very different personality to the person with a penchant for quiet landscapes and Victorian watercolours.

To some extent the space you live in dictates the art you collect: a beach house in Malibu with double-height ceilings, for example, and a cramped studio flat in London would require entirely different collections of art. But you do not need to live in a mansion to display art. One British art collector and lecturer lives on a council estate in north London, in a tiny house crammed with pictures, programmes, postcards and sculptures.

Remember that the art you choose can significantly affect the atmosphere of a room. Close your eyes for a second and imagine that you are looking at the peachy-cheeked subject of an Ingres portrait; then think of the very different feelings evoked by the disturbing, distorted figures of Otto Dix. You get the picture? Some paintings evoke more pleasant emotions than others. Ultimately, you have to be able to live with a piece of art and look at it every day.

at home with art through the ages

The Romans had their frescoes, the Greeks their sculptures, and the Egyptians their gilded statues and papyrus paintings. The 300,000-year-old paintings on the walls of the Chauvet cave in south-east France, which include pictures of mammoths and other ferocious animals, prove that even prehistoric man was partial to embellishing his living space with a little bit of artistic endeavour.

At varying points in time, art within the home has served several different functions. Until the Renaissance, domestic art was rare and its subject was predominantly religious. The trend for portraits in the eighteenth and nineteenth centuries, meanwhile, was a way of recording somebody's likeness for posterity before the invention of photography. Having your portrait painted by a fashionable artist was also a sign of status and wealth: in the 1840s and 1850s wealthy families and influential figures, including the Bonaparte family, were painted by the French artist Jean Auguste Dominique Ingres. This was the nineteenth-century equivalent of having your picture taken today by a top photographer like Patrick Demarchelier.

Art has always been linked with power, status and wealth. During the Renaissance, commissioning artists became a competitive pastime and some rich families went bankrupt in the pursuit of the best interior decoration and art. Artists such as Botticelli and Raphael were employed to decorate the interiors of palaces and homes belonging to popes, princes and wealthy families alike. These Renaissance artists assumed the role of interior decorator, not only producing paintings but overseeing the entire design of a room. It was fashionable to cover every part of the wall with paintings; to adorn ceilings with rosettes and to create niches for sculpture – all characterized by strict symmetry.

Perhaps the most grandiose example of art within a home – albeit a royal palace – is Versailles. During the seventeenth century French painter Charles Le Brun, who was responsible for much of the palace's decoration, used the ornate walls of the grand apartments to act as an appropriately grand backdrop for Louis XIV's collection of Old Master paintings – all hung in formal, symmetrical groups. The effect was one of huge overstatement and splendour. It is a decorative style that is still much copied today and which, in the words of art critic Waldemar Januszczak, 'has become the favoured house style of the nouveaux riches around the globe'.

It was in the seventeenth century, too, that the Dutch bourgeoisie began to embellish their dour homes with portraits by the likes of Jan Vermeer and Rembrandt. The French aristocracy meanwhile, favoured delicately coloured pastorals – of lovers in gardens, for example – and still-lifes by Jean-Honoré Fragonard, François Boucher and Jean-Baptiste Siméon Chardin. These artists were exponents of the Rococo style which, while still one of excess, was a reaction to the formal style of Louis XIV. The graceful and softly coloured works of these artists was appealing to the aristocracy because, unlike history paintings in the grand style, they were designed to add comfort and a feeling of warmth to a domestic environment. Chardin, for example, painted furnishings, crockery and kitchen utensils rather than plump Venuses in the process of bathing. Nevertheless, whatever its subject, art was still very much used as the visible status symbol.

RIGHT: FURNITURE IS USED AS A FORM OF ARTISTIC EXPRESSION, WITH THE CURVY LINES OF ARNE JACOBSEN'S 'SWAN' CHAIR MAKING A BIG IMPACT ON THIS MODERN INTERIOR.

Modernism and a new era in art were ushered in with the twentieth century. Collecting the work of avant-garde or 'challenging' artists became as much a way of demonstrating that you were broad-minded as a conspicuous display of wealth. Pop Art in the 1960s, which was a specific reaction to the elitist, highbrow art of Abstract Expressionism that preceded it, stretched this idea to the limit by proposing that everything which had a place in the world had its place in art, including vacuum cleaners, telephones and fridges. Pop Art also exerted an influence on our taste in interiors and art. The current fascination with loft spaces and large-scale canvases can be traced back to Andy Warhol's Factory, a down-at-heel but buzzy, artistic commune, where he could display his bright, screen-printed canvases to perfection.

trends and changing tastes

Taste in art has changed dramatically throughout history. Take, for example, Aristotle's view. He declared that, 'In painting, the most brilliant colours, spread at random and without design, will give far less pleasure than the simplest outline of a figure.' Obviously, the Greek philosopher did not live to see the big, strong, non-figurative works of such twentieth-century artists as Henri Matisse, Joan Miró or Piet Mondrian, which might well have changed his mind. There are fashions in art as there are with anything, and it's generally true that what is unfashionable today is likely to be fashionable tomorrow. Contemporary art has become extremely fashionable, despite the fact that it often takes a battering from both critics and the general public; it may be simply because people like to buy the art of living artists, the art of their own time. Certain types of art, however – work by the Old Masters, the Impressionists and the established names of the twentieth century – will always be popular and retain their financial value. Collectors are unlikely to ever start off-loading Van Goghs, Renoirs or Cézanne's at bargain prices because these artists have an enduring appeal.

One of the best examples of the whims of artistic taste is Victorian classical art. Forty years ago it was about as fashionable as trainspotting is today, but a painting by Sir Lawrence Alma-Tadema depicting the discovery of Moses in the bullrushes, which in 1950 had been valued at £275, sold in the 1990s for £1.8m. Apparently the painting was bought in 1950 for its frame (the canvas was dumped as rubbish in a Mayfair alley). By 1973 the painting had somehow found its way into the hands of a well-known collector and its most recent sale price confirms that Victorian classical art should no longer be consigned to the art world's rubbish heap.

Certain types of glass, ceramics and textiles, previously classified as crafts, have recently acquired fine-art status, demonstrating how one generation's idea of the mundane can be the next generation's idea of art. It is all about challenging the perceptions of the day. The humble quilt is one such functional object which has become a work of art. How did it happen? It is more than likely that the geometric work of modern artists opened our eyes to the artistic merit of intricate patterns and colours. Equally, you may laugh at the vulgar figurines advertised in Sunday newspaper supplements, but it is possible that future generations might consider them collectable. The moral is clear: whatever you like – be it teapots or toy cars – is irrelevant. It is up to future generations to decide whether or not it may be considered as art.

the pleasure principle

We have all heard the stories about the lucky soul who picked up a Picasso sketch in a garage sale for 50p and then sold it for £20,000. But art should not be bought with a view to making money. The best reason for buying a painting is the fact that you love it and you could happily look at it for the rest of your life. It is true that money can be made through shrewd buying and selling. Renoir's *La Promenade* is one famous example: it was sold for £680,000 in 1976 and for £9.4 million in 1989. Gallery-bought art can be a valuable investment as well as adding character and style to an interior. But buying art is a lottery. It is far better to view it as a way of keeping a visual diary of your life – a reflection of your tastes and personality at different times – rather than something that will boost your bank account. When buying a painting, your main consideration should be whether you find the image appealing. At the end of the day it is all a matter of taste. And the only taste that counts is yours.

the art of the future

What of the art of the future? Video installations and conceptual art – everything from footage of Las Vegas casinos to piles of oranges on the floor – are becoming commonplace, but it is difficult to see how they fit into the domestic environment. Design guru Stephen Bayley predicted a move away from this genre of art: 'People will become more interested in proper art rather than conceptual Turner-prize stuff and take pleasure in owning something individual,' he says. More interesting, still, is the way Bayley sees art being sold in the future: Maintaining that we will avoid buying at commercial galleries and 'Go to places … that show and sell art within a family home' certainly makes sense. After all, stores selling designer furniture show their customers mocked-up room sets to serve as inspiration, so why shouldn't art dealers take this to its logical conclusion? The downside to this would be a reduction of the pleasure derived from buying a piece of art. After all, the real fun starts when you take your artwork home and try to work out how best to fit it into your surroundings.

home is where the art is

Although you should not be precious about art in the home, you do want to show a piece to its best advantage – whether it be a Warhol poster or an original Pissarro painting. This does not mean that you have to make your home resemble a museum, however, or even coordinate your upholstery with the painting. What it does mean is that you should make every effort to put the painting in the right frame and find the best position for it. Remember, when you look at the homes featured in glossy newspaper supplements for inspiration, that the apparently random arrangements have almost certainly been 'styled' with meticulous attention to detail. Whether a room features a solitary sculpture, or is hung with pictures from ceiling to floor, the impact often depends on getting the small details and practicalities right – as the rest of this book will demonstrate. In all of this, one thing remains certain: living with art today is a far more complex affair (and more fun) than simply hammering in a couple of picture hooks before hanging a painted canvas on the wall.

the practicalities

'anything goes with anything'

ANDY WARHOL

THE ART OF LIVING

There are many ways of incorporating art in the contemporary home, but creating the right surroundings to show off a piece to its best advantage is an art in itself. The background colour scheme, the lighting and the positioning of the piece are just a few of the practical considerations that can enhance your enjoyment of a painting or artwork. How does the painting work with your furniture, for example? Does it 'fight' with another picture on the same wall, or does it enhance it? Remember that, in any arrangement, the individual pieces will affect one another and the result can either be jarring or pleasing. This does not mean, however, that you have to match a painting to your upholstery, or worry that a tangerine-coloured abstract will clash with your tranquil decor. As Andy Warhol once said: 'Anything goes with anything.'

Art in the home is an entirely different entity to art in a museum or gallery and consequently it is subject to a different set of considerations. After all, you have to live with it, and not just gaze at it momentarily as you pass through a room. You might wonder how serious collectors live with their art. How do millionaires who own a Rembrandt, a Monet or a Picasso display it at home? The truth is that many of the world's leading collectors do not live with their masterpieces at all. Often these works travel the world, by kind permission of their owners, on loan to galleries and museums. Equally, having built up a collection, a family might donate it under their name to a national institution.

Many collectors who have deep pockets simply cannot stop buying and end up with a surfeit of art. They are then forced either to keep a large part of their collection in storage or to build museum-quality storage within their home. Swiss count Thyssen-Bornemisza had his collection of twentieth-century masters mounted on rolling screens and filed in the basement of his museum in Basel; British advertising guru Charles Saatchi used a converted paint factory to display his canvases. Certain collectors might purchase conceptual art purely as a financial investment, yet have no desire to display a large-scale installation, or a sculpture of a bloodied head, for example, in their homes. Other art connoisseurs end up remodelling their homes in order to accommodate their collection, ripping down walls, enlarging hallways and destroying rooms in order to create large expanses of space. One American collector even bricked up a row of windows in his apartment to create more hanging space, while another built a warehouse measuring 56 square metres (6,000 square feet) in his garden to house his burgeoning collection.

Collectors who own more than one home can afford the luxury of expressing their different tastes in art in each of them. Terence Conran, the king of contemporary furnishings, is a good example. Most people

assume that he has ruthlessly modern taste in furniture and art, but in fact, the eighteenth-century house he owns in the country is filled with antique furniture, old family portraits and paintings by Sir Joshua Reynolds. Similarly, one famous American couple who also collect art have two homes, each housing a very different collection. Their principal residence is a modern beach house in Hawaii, which they have filled with colourful modern art. An old farmhouse in Vermont, their second home, is packed with folksy pieces and all kinds of clutter reflecting the art of the region. Most of us, of course, have just one home and do not have to worry about where to house a large collection.

In stark contrast to the nineteenth century, when it was fashionable to cram as much into a room as possible – antiques, carpets, furniture, ornately framed paintings and patterned wallpaper – recent decor concentrates on the less-is-more dictum, to the point where many modern interiors resemble white, empty museum spaces. Trends usually run to opposite extremes, however, so who knows what might happen in the not-too-distant future. We may well decide to revert to elaborate interiors and want masses of antiques and art with which to furnish our space.

insurance

It should be possible to insure a piece of art costing less than a £1,000 on your existing household contents policy. If you have lots of valuable furniture or paintings, however, or even a family heirloom, you might want to take out a separate policy from a company that specializes in insuring art. It is also a good idea to prepare an inventory of the art that you own and to keep a visual record of it – either by taking Polaroid pictures or by making a video tape. This will facilitate identification and help to prove ownership if anything is ever stolen.

INSTALLING AND ARRANGING ART

space and proportions

It is important to consider how an artwork will suit its space. Most people buy art simply because they like it, and while you should never purchase a piece just to fill a space, or force it to coordinate with a colour scheme, it is a good idea to think about the room where you intend to put it. To use an obvious example, Damien Hirst's big blue tank with a pickled shark might work beautifully in a modern loft space but would appear ludicrous in a small terraced house. As a rule, modern art works best with clean-lined contemporary furniture, while older art benefits from period furnishings and formal surroundings. Rules, however, are made to be broken, and a modern poster or print is more than at home, for example, in a Georgian drawing room, particularly if the room in question is sparsely decorated and furnished with contemporary pieces.

Artworks on a smaller scale benefit from being in a smaller room – such as a lobby or hallway – where they can be viewed at close proximity, and outsized works generally need high ceilings to be displayed to their best advantage. If you are lucky enough to own a home that is big enough to accommodate larger-scale paintings and sculpture, you might also want to consider scaling up the furniture in order to keep things in proportion. But, once again, you can break the rules: there is no reason why a large-scale canvas cannot be hung floor-to-ceiling in a smaller space, or even used to fill an entire wall. Some pictures deserve space and get lost if they are crowded on a wall with other pictures; others require an entire wall to themselves. It is only by playing around with pictures, and perhaps living with them for a while, that you will figure out what will and will not work. When installing art, you should consider how it looks both close up and from a distance – even from other rooms. Sculptures and collectable pieces of furniture ideally need space around them so they can be viewed from all sides – unless they are flat or two-dimensional.

BELOW: THE ADVANTAGE OF PROPPING A CANVAS IN A HALLWAY OR SMALL SPACE IS THAT IT CAN BE VIEWED AT CLOSE PROXIMITY.

BELOW: LARGE-SCALE PIECES OF
FURNITURE OR ART NEED SPACE
AROUND THEM TO ENABLE THEM
TO 'BREATHE'.

the power of one piece

Collecting art does not mean owning enough paintings or objects to open your own gallery and charge your friends an entrance fee! Often the most striking way to feature art at home is to display one beautiful piece prominently. Less really does seem to be more. Imagine, for example, a simple white sculpture recessed in a lilac wall behind a bed in an otherwise minimalist bedroom; or a Mies van der Rohe chair in a room largely stripped of furniture; or a colourful Kandinsky print neatly centred above the fireplace in a Georgian sitting room or a modern loft. It might be worthwhile saving up for one really good original painting or a limited-edition print rather than several inferior pieces. If you stick to a few carefully chosen pieces and keep the rest of the interior decor simple, it is fine to mix furniture from different periods for a contemporary look. At the end of the day, the glue that holds a mixed collection together is the passion and personality of the person who compiled it.

LEFT: THE STRIKING RED LEATHER GLOVE SOFA – VIEWED THROUGH THE BARS OF THE STAIR RAILINGS – ACTS AS THE FOCAL POINT IN THIS INTERIOR.

TOP RIGHT: *TREES, HALLOWEEN* (2000) – OIL ON CANVAS BY MARC HULSON, FEATURED IN THE HOME-CUM-GALLERY OF ART DEALER DANIELLE ARNAUD, OWNER OF THE CONTEMPORARY ART GALLERY.

RIGHT: *WITNESS* (1999), AN INSTALLATION BY SUSAN MORRIS.

symmetry and asymmetry

When you have decided to make a feature of the art in your home, it is important to consider the serious question of symmetry. A symmetrical arrangement is the most formal way to display art. Such an arrangement helps to create a sense of order but is also easy on the eye – whether it is a painting hung dead centre over a fireplace, two vases positioned at either end of a mantelpiece, or half a dozen small pictures arranged in a neat rectangular placement. Some *objets d'art*, like antique vases, look better (and are more valuable) in pairs.

That said, an asymmetrical placement can also have great impact, whether it is a series of prints of different sizes dotted randomly on a wall, or a canvas placed deliberately off-centre above a fireplace. Generally, it is large canvases and bold modern works – such as the graffiti-like scrawls of a Cy Twombly, the random splatterings of a Jackson Pollock or a geometric square of Yves Klein colour – that lend themselves to this adventurous hanging style. You could also play around with different shapes and sizes of canvas on the same wall. Most paintings, drawings or framed paintings are square or rectangular but you can add circular canvases – such as Damien Hirst's *Spin* pictures or Robert Delaunay's circular paintings – to interesting effect.

LEFT: AN ASYMMETRICAL PLACEMENT CAN HAVE GREAT IMPACT. HERE, A METAL BLOCK SCULPTURE HAS BEEN DELIBERATELY PLACED OFF-CENTRE IN A HOME DESIGNED BY ARCHITECT JONATHAN REED.

RIGHT: THE BEST THINGS COME IN PAIRS – IN THIS CASE A SYMMETRICAL ARRANGEMENT OF TWO 'TONGUE CHAIRS' BY PIERRE PAULIN.

colour and background

Many people assume that because white is often the background of choice in galleries and museums, it is the best colour for displaying art at home. While it is true that white walls and bare floorboards reflect light and can brilliantly off-set both deeply coloured carpets and/or paintings, there is no reason why you should restrict yourself to cream walls, furniture and curtains. The predilection for cream or pale grey in galleries is largely due to practical considerations: neutral colours are the easiest to maintain against the impact of ever-changing displays. In a domestic setting, dark or bright wall colours can increase the impact of a display of paintings, so be bold when you are choosing your background colour. Then live with it for a while. If you don't like it, you can always re-paint. And remember, you can afford to be most adventurous with colour in the rooms you use least frequently – the spare room, for instance, or the dining room where you spend less time.

shelving and display cabinets

Shelving is much more than a functional means of housing a collection. It can really enhance a display of objects. Glass shelves always look stylish but there are many other options: thick black-lacquer shelving, for instance, is ideal for a collection of oriental vases or modern ceramics, while intricate 1970s-style white 'Faro' wall bricks are an innovative way to display glassware. Customized shelving is another option, where shelves are built to fit the space available – whether it is a cubbyhole under the stairs or an expanse of living-room wall. Good lighting is crucial for both recessed and open shelving. A colourful collection of Murano glass, for example, looks even more beautiful displayed on backlit shelving.

Making a highlight of a single sculpture or vase in a wall recess is also striking. During the Renaissance artists commissioned to provide the overall decorative scheme for a room would construct special niches to house sculptures and statues. Arched or – more modern – rectangular recesses are still one of the most effective means of drawing attention to a single object. You can also light a recess dramatically or paint it in a colour that contrasts with the rest of the wall to draw the eye inwards.

Fragile, easily damaged objects will benefit from the protection of a glass display case. This is also a neat way to contain collections of objects such as scent bottles, ceramics or Tonka toys, and prevent them from cluttering up other surfaces. Relatively inexpensive display cabinets can be easily sourced from contemporary furniture stores like Ikea and Heal's, and you will find that their modern streamlined design will fit unobtrusively into any contemporary interior.

ABOVE: WOODEN BOWLS HAVE ARTISTIC MERIT WHEN DISPLAYED WITH FLAIR.

ABOVE RIGHT: GOOD SHELVING CAN ENHANCE A DISPLAY OF OBJECTS.

OPPOSITE: DANIELLE ARNAUD'S HOME GALLERY (TOP), LEFT TO RIGHT: ZURICH BY JERRY SMITH, (1997) OIL ON CANVAS; UNTITLED BY MARIE-NOELLE FALTICSKA (1998), PIGMENT ON PAPER; BODY BY MARIE-FRANCE AND PATRICIA MARTIN (1988), PHOTOGRAPH. MARIE-NOELLE FALTICSKA'S UNTITLED PIGMENT ON PAPER WORKS WELL AGAINST A YELLOW BACKGROUND (BOTTOM).

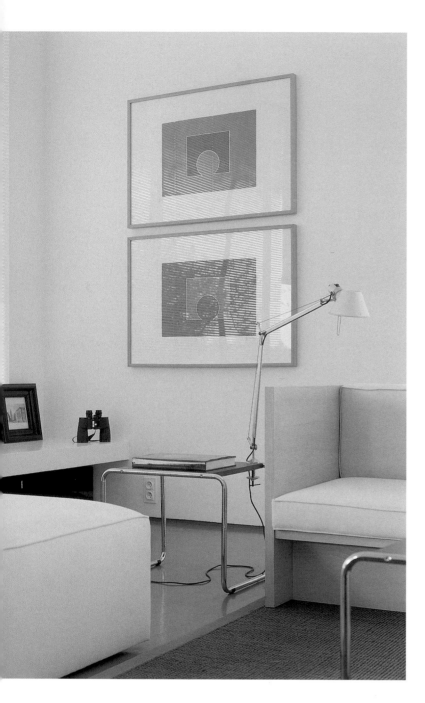

ABOVE: IT IS IMPORTANT TO CONSIDER
WHERE THE LIGHT WILL FALL WHEN
HANGING AND LIGHTING WORKS OF ART.

OPPOSITE: LIGHTING ART HAS ITSELF
BECOME AN ART, WITH MORE INNOVATIVE
TECHNIQUES – IN THIS CASE, LIGHTING
RECESSED INTO THE CEILING – REPLACING
THE OLD-FASHIONED PICTURE LIGHT.

shedding light on the subject

Just as you can alter the ambience of a room with the flick of a light switch, so you can transform a painting by the way that you light it. Gilded frames were used in the past because the gold reflected the candlelight and drew attention to the picture. Today, there are many more devices and variable lighting methods available and you can use different kinds of light to accent objects and paintings in different ways. Lighting should always take into account the distance from which the art will be viewed and you should consider exactly where the light should fall.

Natural light is best for viewing art but the ultraviolet rays contained in direct sunlight can damage or fade textiles, oils and works on paper. Serious collectors rotate fragile pieces of art – drawings, prints, photographs – displaying them for short periods in direct sunlight and then moving them to an area that receives only indirect light. Different paintings also have different lighting requirements. A dark and moody Rembrandt will require more direct lighting than a Gustav Klimt containing touches of reflective gold, for example. While in a museum everything is lit for clarity, at home you can use more atmospheric lighting and then supplement it with focused light sources.

The old-fashioned picture light, comprising a tubular bulb attached to the frame over the painting, provides evenly spread light but is considered both pretentious and only suitable for traditional paintings. While serious collectors sometimes install sophisticated and costly lighting systems, the humble spotlight is a simple and effective way to highlight a contemporary work of art. It can be fitted to the ceiling or walls, or used on a floor stand. Ceiling-mounted tracking is relatively inexpensive and versatile, too, because individual spotlights can be moved to highlight any work of art in a room. The drawback to tracking is that it is not compatible with older-style interiors.

Portable up-lighters and table lamps create a softer, more diffused light, while halogen lighting provides a concentrated and precise beam. There is much to be said for the brilliance of halogen bulbs, but be warned: if a bulb is placed too close to a painting, the heat might harm the fabric.

Concealed lighting is one of the best ways of illuminating objects on shelves or in a recess. Fluorescent tubes or low-voltage fittings with reflectors, for example, can be hidden behind or above shelves to create magical and theatrical effects. Certain light fixtures are, in themselves, an art form (see pages 144–7) and when placed under or adjacent to a painting, will create atmospheric lighting.

A ROOM-BY-ROOM GUIDE TO USING ART

introduction

Nudes in the bathroom; erotica in the bedroom; Impressionist landscapes in the living room; and paintings of fruit and vegetables in the kitchen: these are the most predictable art-in-room combinations. Traditionally, collectors will display their most treasured pieces in the sitting room or dining room, where guests can admire them. But it is worth thinking beyond the obvious. Any room in the house can act as a backdrop for art. A big print of an artichoke has increased impact hung above a bed, for example, because of the unexpectedness of its location. Similarly, imagine the effect of a nude drawing in the kitchen, a collection of kitchen ceramics displayed in the bathroom, or an arrangement of antique scent bottles in the sitting room.

Nevertheless, there are practical considerations to take into account. While it would be exceptionally understated to hang a drawing by Picasso in the bathroom, for example, it would also be most unwise to do so because of the possibility of steam damage.

RIGHT: THE CLEAN LINES OF THIS
BLACK-AND-WHITE ABSTRACT ARE
PERFECTLY IN KEEPING WITH THIS
MODERNIST BATHROOM.

'I love nothing more than unwinding in the bath, looking at all my framed black-and-white photographs.' Nina Campbell, interior designer.

the bathroom

The bathroom is not an obvious place to feature art, especially oil paintings or fragile works on paper, because of the heat, steam and humidity. It is, however, a good spot for a small sculpture, a ceramic or a collection of perfume bottles, shells or glass. One of the most striking displays of glass that I have ever seen was in the home of a fashion model in Miami. The bathroom, in direct contrast to the rest of the minimal white apartment, boasted a beautiful and unexpected collection of colourful glass fish by Lalique, arranged on a glass shelf above the washbasin.

Posters of water or shower scenes – a particular preoccupation of Pop artists such as Tom Wesselman and David Hockney – make for witty additions to the washroom. Hockney's scene of two men in a shower might be a little too suggestive for some tastes but his Hollywood paintings, which feature swimming pools and palm trees, evoke dream-like idylls and are relaxing to look at while you are languishing in the tub. Framed photographs are also good wallowing material, and work well in the bathroom. Toothpaste tubes were another icon of the Pop Art era. With its clear colours and blue tones, Derek Boshier's *First Toothpaste Painting* (1962), makes the perfect piece of bathroom art.

The smallest room in the house, meanwhile, makes the ideal site for a mosaic – the art form featured in the bath houses and villas of the ancient Romans. Pictorial mosaics are very expensive to install (see page 72) and probably require the services of a professional artist. You could, however, create an artistic effect in the manner of a mosaic by placing coloured tiles randomly within a white-tiled wall or floor.

the kitchen

Food has always been seen as an inspirational subject for art, from the luscious apricots, plums and crusty loaves of Jean-Baptiste Chardin's nineteenth-century still-lifes to the menu of cakes, cola bottles and ice creams favoured by Pop artists. In the contemporary home, however, the exuberance of a Pop Art poster looks more in keeping than a still-life of a dead pheasant. Art in the kitchen should be fun, upbeat and a little bit quirky. Andy Warhol's bananas or Campbell's soup cans are just the right ingredients for contemporary kitchen art. Prints of *EAT or DIE* by American Pop artist Robert Indiana are good examples, too. Or maybe you could opt for a bold, graphic picture of a single fruit or vegetable. You could even make up your own words or follow the lead of Jean-Michel Basquiat and indulge in a little blackboard art by making a feature of shopping lists or messages. In many family homes, the fridge door is given over to children's paintings, pinned in place with magnets. The grown-up version of fridge art is to cover a pinboard or cupboard door with art postcards and inspirational pictures of mouth-watering foods or recipes torn from magazines. But the kitchen is not the place to hang serious paintings or oils as they are likely to get damaged by steam and grease. Choose posters and pictures framed under Plexiglass, which can be easily cleaned.

LEFT: CAMPBELL'S SOUP CANS AND JACK DANIELS' BOTTLES CREATE A POP-ART INSPIRED DISPLAY IN THIS KITCHEN.

ABOVE: PRINTS OF *EAT* OR *DIE* BY AMERICAN POP ARTIST ROBERT INDIANA ADD A QUIRKY NOTE TO THIS DINING AREA.

the sitting or dining room

The sitting room lends itself to a display of art of all kinds – paintings, ceramics, wall hangings, vases and carpets – because this is where most people will see and enjoy it. As the room in which you are most likely to relax and entertain guests, it is the obvious place to display your favourite or most expensive work of art. The pictures that you hang here will affect the ambiance of the whole room, so if you want to create an upbeat, friendly atmosphere, a poster of Edvard Munch's *The Scream* is not ideal. A colourful Matisse print or a Patrick Caulfield poster, on the other hand, instantly strikes a modern, playful note. Groups of objects, displayed either on shelves or in special glass cases, also look good in a sitting room, although it is worth bearing in mind that it is more appealing to have a few well-chosen books displayed on a coffee table or to intersperse objects and books with small pictures propped up on shelves than to have every available surface piled high with books and *objets d'art*.

LEFT: TREAT A ROOM ALMOST AS A COMPOSITION. IN THIS CASE, AN EILEEN GRAY TABLE FLANKED BY TWO MODERN CHAIRS CREATES PERFECT SYMMETRY WITH THE TWO OIL PAINTINGS ON THE WALL.

RIGHT: THE SITTING ROOM IS THE IDEAL PLACE TO DISPLAY A COLLECTION OF CERAMICS, BUT REMEMBER: LESS IS MORE.

the bedroom

The bedroom is the ideal place to hang more personal paintings and framed photographs. If you prefer to be surrounded by more seductive artworks in your bedroom, you could choose a voluptuous nude, or the erotic black-and-white photographs of Helmut Newton or Jeanloupe Sieff. Alternatively, you could even make your own bedroom collage, inspired by Peter Blake's *Love Wall* (1961), which features postcards of red hearts and black-and-white pictures of Hollywood movie icons locked in a series of romantic clinches.

For a non-traditional approach, you could create visual impact either by hanging a hand-painted piece of fabric on the wall above the bed, or by making a still-life using accessories or clothes. Suggestions include displaying a beautiful shoe on a wall, hanging colourful jewellery from a nail, or draping a favourite dress on a hanger and suspending it from the ceiling with a ribbon. Some collectors save their favourite pieces for the bedroom so that they can look at them first thing in the morning and last thing at night. If you want your bedroom to be a haven of serenity, however, you should steer clear of challenging, violent or angst-ridden pieces of work which might provoke nightmares. Instead, opt for restful, soothing or seductive paintings that literally invite the eye to slip into something more comfortable.

LEFT: THE BEDROOM IS THE IDEAL
PLACE TO HANG EROTIC ARTWORKS:
THIS PHOTOGRAPH BY MIRA BERNABEU
IN THE BEDROOM OF JIBBY BEANE'S SELF-
DESIGNED APARTMENT IN CLERKENWELL,
LONDON, IS THE PERFECT EXAMPLE.

hallways and staircases

The artwork that you put in the hallway creates the first impression guests receive of your home, which is why fashionable advertising agencies and banks often boast huge, modern works of art in their reception areas. Hallways are the perfect spaces to hang pictures and, if long or wide enough, they can become almost like galleries. Small hallways have the advantage of offering a greater degree of intimacy with a painting or object. A canvas viewed from afar can take on a whole new meaning when viewed up close. In a narrow hallway, you will be able to contemplate the texture and patina, and discern every brushstroke of an oil painting. The hall is a good spot to put an interesting sculpture or small-scale installation, and it often makes the perfect shaded home for fragile artworks that would otherwise suffer damage from direct sunlight.

The staircase is another ideal place for pictures. A series of prints by the same artist, or framed black-and-white fine-art photographs leading up the wall will entice the eye upwards.

ABOVE: HANGING PICTURES IN A HALLWAY
CAN CREATE AN ART-GALLERY FEEL.

RIGHT: THE ARTWORK THAT YOU
HANG IN YOUR HALLWAY IS VERY
IMPORTANT AS IT WILL CREATE THE
FIRST IMPRESSION THAT VISITORS
WILL HAVE OF YOUR HOME.

COMMISSIONING A PIECE OF ART

Art made to order – in consultation with the artist – is the ultimate way to buy. Portraits are the most sought-after and popular form of commissioned art. Few can afford the £500,000-plus that it would cost to commission a portrait by Lucian Freud but it is possible to find younger artists at college degree shows, catching them before fame jacks their prices into the stratosphere.

Commissioning a portrait is the most usual way to start but remember that you can also order furniture, sculpture and carpets made to your own specifications. The advantage of commissioned art is that you can control the end result and ensure that it suits your surroundings. In addition, you will also have created something you can pass on to future generations.

Commissioning art need not be expensive but it can become addictive. Visit galleries, annual exhibitions and graduate shows to look for designers whose work you like. At such events you can chat with the artist or maker informally, without making a commitment. As far as commissioning furniture or carpets goes, the creative input can come from both sides, although it is important to admire the core work of the artist you are commissioning. Obviously, you cannot be so precise with paintings because the artist will expect his or her creative genius to be given free reign.

Work out what you want, where you want it to go and a budget before briefing the artist. Ideally, he or she should visit you at home to discuss your requirements and to view the surroundings in which the art will be placed, as well as getting a feel for your personality. If you are commissioning a piece of furniture, you will be shown preliminary drawings, but in return you will probably be asked to make staggered payments for time and materials. As the work progresses, it is a good idea to telephone and visit the artist or maker to check on the progress of the piece from time to time.

LEFT: COMMISSIONING A PIECE OF ART
ENSURES THAT THE WORK RELATES
DIRECTLY TO ITS SURROUNDINGS.

site-specific art

Most pieces of art today – commissioned or otherwise – are portable. But it is possible to commission an artist to paint directly onto your walls, or to create a sculpture or feature that will become an integral part of the structure of your home. Trompe-l'oeil murals creating fake vistas of country gardens or ocean-front views are typical examples of site-specific art. The obvious drawback of art that is part of the wall, ceiling or floor is that it can only be moved with difficulty and/or great expense. It is best to view such art as ephemeral, and not as something that you will be able to carry with you for the rest of your life.

hang it all

'an image
has to be beautiful
to be effective'

JEANLOUP SIEFF, PHOTOGRAPHER

ART FOR THE HOME

The word 'art' to most people means a painting hanging on a wall.
Indeed, this is by far the most popular way to feature art in the home.
But there are many other forms of two-dimensional art. Think of the
new generation of patterned wallpapers, for example, or the ethereal
images that gallery owner Jibby Beane likes to project on to the walls
of her home. People are becoming generally more inventive in the way
they decorate their walls – using advertising billboard posters to paper
the walls of lofts, or mounting light boxes to display family snaps in the
living room of a Victorian home. Think of your walls as a giant canvas:
you can paint directly onto them, or create patterns with different
types of wallpaper. Wall art comes in many different guises and even
the colour of paint that you choose is part of the artistic effect.

PAINTINGS AND CANVASES

picture perfect

It is always best to buy an original, whatever the constraints of your budget, as there is always the chance that one day it may be considered a masterpiece. Art is more accessible than you might think, and although not everyone can afford a Renoir or a Lucian Freud, many serious collectors begin by buying prints, posters, drawings and lithographs. You can buy a lithograph or limited-edition print by a well-known artist for less than £500. For the same amount of money you will be able to acquire a reasonable watercolour or drawing; and £1,000 will buy you an original by a fairly well-respected artist. At a Christie's contemporary art sale preview recently, I was amazed to discover that it is still possible to buy an oil painting by Claude Monet for the price of a car (£20,000). Admittedly, it was a lesser-known and inferior work, but it was a Monet nonetheless!

It is quite possible, over a period of years, to assemble a creditable collection without spending huge amounts of money. The trick is to catch artists before they become fashionable, because as soon as somebody is patronized by a dealer or trendy gallery such as Whitecube in London, the price of a painting can rocket from £1,000 to £20,000 almost overnight. Collectors of Pop Art in the 1950s and 1960s, for example, were able to build up big collections for peanuts, because at that time few people understood such works and the desire to own them was minimal. Nowadays, we are becoming increasingly clued up, and the media hype around young artists can send prices into orbit.

The golden rule is to collect for pleasure rather than investment – acquiring a painting because you simply have to have it. Many people find that their tastes change over time. As Antony Thorncroft wrote in the *Financial Times*: 'Often you start with colourful, decorative, figurative paintings. Then you go for more challenging images. Finally, you might end up scouring the studios of the conceptualists and the installationists.' Whatever your tastes, remember to follow your instincts and only buy something you would be happy to look at every day.

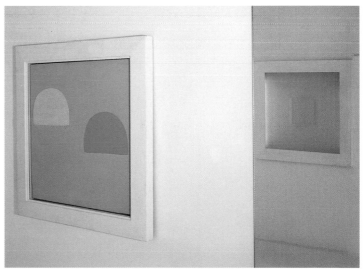

LEFT: THE GEOMETRIC SHAPES IN THIS ARTWORK, WHICH HAS BEEN PAINTED DIRECTLY ONTO THE WALL, REFLECT THE CLEAN, ANGULAR LINES OF THE ROOM.

ABOVE: COLOUR – IN THIS CASE, SKY BLUE AGAINST A WHITE FRAME AND WALL – PROVIDES THE IMPACT OF THESE GRAPHIC IMAGES.

in the frame

The fun really begins after you have bought a painting. You may have purchased it with a frame or you may just have bought the canvas – either way, framing a picture correctly is crucial, in both historic and aesthetic terms. The National Gallery in London, for example, spent ten years sourcing the right frame for Turner's *Rain, Steam and Speed*. It is partly a question of subtlety, both as regards colour and carving, because the wrong frame can ruin a picture.

The first and most important consideration is the period in which a painting was executed, and the widely-held view that an old picture should only be teamed with a frame of the same period holds fast: an Old Master painting, full of rich, dark colours for example, would look very wrong in a modern, pale-wood frame (fashionable though it is to put modern pictures in older-looking surrounds).

Certain pictures, because of their value and age, seem to demand highly ornate, gilded frames, but there are lots to choose from and the price range is wide. Some framers will visit a client at home to get an idea of the picture's proposed background. If you are unsure, it is worth asking your framer if this service is an option. Ultimately, the value of the picture should dictate, to some extent, whether you need an antique frame or a modern reproduction (there is no point in paying three times as much for the frame as you did for the painting). Remember, though, that the right surround can really enhance a picture. 'I love watching the expression on people's faces when you show the difference the right frame makes,' says Paul Mitchell, a London specialist in antique frames. Some ornate frames have such artistic merit you can simply leave it empty and prop it against a brightly coloured wall (gilded wood looks especially good against cornflower blue or lilac).

You can afford to be more adventurous with contemporary pictures or posters, partly because the choice available is more diverse – although simple styles such as pale wood or silver metal frames remain the most popular. Both of these types make effective frames for modern abstracts and poster art, while black or walnut-effect surrounds look very stylish with black-and-white prints or photographs. Large departments stores sell good-quality black, Plexiglas frames which are great for pictures that you want to frame yourself. Posters might not need a frame at all – just a piece of Plexiglas and some simple clips.

There are many more adventurous options for those with deep pockets. Rollo Whately, a London framer whose clients include interior designer Nicky Haslam and chef Marco Pierre White, sells some of the most contemporary surrounds available (he recently sourced a green Perspex frame which originally enclosed a work by David Hockney),

and is one of many dealers who view frames as a work of art in their own right. There are no limits to the colours or materials that can be used other than the imagination. Remember to keep an open mind when you take your picture to the framer as he or she may well suggest something you hadn't thought of, but which could look fantastic.

The medium and brushwork of a painting can also dictate the type of surround. The heavy, textured strokes of Lucian Freud's paintings, for example, are shown to their best advantage in dark, distressed wooden frames, while Tracey Emin's framed magazine and newspaper pages look best in blonde, wooden box frames, which are almost three-dimensional and have a museum-display effect.

You can, of course, eschew contemporary surrounds altogether: a decorative, nineteenth-century frame can lend gravitas to a modern picture. Hans Roeder of London framers F A Pollack often pairs modern masters with sixteenth-or seventeenth-century frames. 'A Braque in

a bold seventeenth-century frame is a splendid thing,' he says. While few people can afford a Braque, the same principle can be applied to a poster. Moreover, antique surrounds are now recognized as not only beautiful but also valuable in their own right.

BELOW: SIMPLE MODERN SURROUNDS GIVE UNIFORMITY TO A MASS OF FRAMED PHOTOGRAPHS.

RIGHT: THE ASYMMETRIC ARRANGEMENT AND MAD MIX OF ORNATE FRAMES IS STRIKINGLY EFFECTIVE ON THIS LAVENDER COLOURED WALL.

HOW TO CHOOSE THE RIGHT FRAME

- Visit museums and galleries for inspiration.
- Bear in mind the other frames in the room or on the wall where the painting will hang, but do not try too hard to match the frame to the decorative style of the room – you might, after all, decide to move the painting at a later date.
- Oil paintings usually require much more ornate frames than watercolours and prints of the same period.
- Glass is essential to protect works on paper and textiles but oil paintings lose something when viewed through glass.
- In general, the more modern the picture, the simpler and more severe the frame can, and perhaps should, be.
- For contemporary paintings and graphics, use pale, polished wooden frames of ash or pine or light maple. Depending on your taste, and the size of the painting, these can be quite heavy – maybe 7.5–10 cm (3–4 in) deep.
- Consider a boxed frame for modern drawings and less conventional pieces. The art is literally boxed into a frame, with the glass standing about 2.5 cm (1 in) above the surface of the picture.
- A frame should enhance the picture within it, not dominate it.
- Do not use an overly ornate frame on an old painting; even if the style is historically authentic, it might overwhelm the piece. It is probably better to choose a very plain, unadorned gold frame instead.
- Play around with different widths, weights, tones and textures before you decide on a frame.

go hang

The most obvious place to hang a painting is above a fireplace – the focal point in most sitting rooms – or above a bed or a chest of drawers in a bedroom. There are no hard-and-fast rules, however, so you could, for example, hang a painting at table height if there is a table next to the wall. Many people like to hang their favourite painting so that it is the first thing they see as they come into a room.

Nevertheless, there are one or two definite no-nos when it comes to hanging watercolours or oil paintings. Never position these paintings above a radiator, in a humid atmosphere, or anywhere where there are draughts. Changes in temperature will cause the canvas or paper to expand and contract, and eventually to flake or crack. Direct sunlight is also harmful to many paintings as it causes them to fade. Also, try to avoid hanging a painting near a door, which could bang into it.

displaying pictures to their best advantage

While it might sound mad to decorate a room around a painting, on reflection there seems no good reason not to – particularly if the picture in question is an old favourite. Fabric designer and interiors specialist Cath Kidston often uses a painting or rug as her point of departure when she is choosing the colours for a room. Indeed, the lilac and mint green colour scheme in the bedroom of her Gloucestershire home was inspired by the colours of a portrait given to her by her great-aunt.

A stark white wall is often the most obvious background for a colourful abstract modern painting, although in some museums the exact opposite is true – with flamboyant works such as the colourful abstracts of Paul Klee or Wassily Kandinsky on muted grey walls, and (in the case of Tate Britain) moody, sombre-coloured pieces, such as J M W Turner are displayed against colourful pinks.

Visiting museums and galleries, and looking at the colours of the walls on which they have chosen to display paintings can often be inspirational. For example, the muted lilac and grey hues chosen as the backdrop for the recent Ingres portrait exhibition at the Metropolitan Museum of Art in New York created a direct contrast to the vivid colours and patterns of the gowns worn by the artist's female subjects, and proved particularly effective.

To show off a painting to its best advantage, a very good ploy is to isolate a colour from the canvas and incorporate it into the decor of the room, even if it is just in a cushion or a vase. Alternatively, you could take the dominant shade in a picture and then decorate the wall on which it

will be displayed in a colour from the opposite spectrum. For example, one of David Hockney's famous Californian swimming pool paintings, or an abstract canvas featuring blue as the dominant shade, would really stand out well against a red wall.

There are signs that museums and galleries are becoming more adventurous in their use of colour and moving away from minimalist white. Architect Richard MacCormac recently chose a mad selection of coloured paint and tinted spotlights to create different moods for a Ruskin exhibition at the Tate. He chose a damson shade, which he christened 'hippy purple', and lit it with tangerine to evoke a feeling of madness. He even hung a group of pre-Raphaelite paintings against black walls. 'Strangely enough, I think black is a good colour to hang pictures against,' he declared. The moral? There are no rules when it comes to art.

LEFT: THIS WALL IS THE IDEAL PLACE
TO HANG A PICTURE. NOTE ALSO
HOW THE ARTWORK IS PERFECTLY
PROPORTIONED FOR THE SPACE.

RIGHT: THE LAID-BACK APPROACH TO
DISPLAYING ART IS TO SIMPLY PROP
A PICTURE ON THE FLOOR, OR ON TOP
OF A PIECE OF FURNITURE.

off the wall

Pictures and prints do not necessarily need to be hung on a wall. Perhaps because some people find the art of picture-hanging deeply stressful (all those pencilled crosses and the noisy drilling), it has become extremely fashionable simply to prop pictures up against a wall. This is a very laid-back way to display artworks, and helps to dissipate some of the 'preciousness' that surrounds art – even though, when a picture seems to have been propped insouciantly against a wall, the effect is probably the result of artful contriving.

Displaying groups of small pictures on shelves is also very effective. Alternatively, you can lie small prints flat on a coffee table, or stand a painting in front of a fireplace instead of hanging it above as an alternative focal point for a room. You could even prop an unframed canvas on a chair, or display it on an easel to suggest that it is still a work in progress. There is something very appealing about the makeshift, informal simplicity of displaying art in this way.

RIGHT: THIS LARGE-SCALE CANVAS
FEATURING A FLOWER IMAGE IS
VERY EFFECTIVE, LEFT LEANING
AGAINST A WALL.

FAR RIGHT: NOTICE HOW WELL THE
FRAMES OF THESE BLACK-AND-WHITE
PHOTOGRAPHS – SEEMINGLY PROPPED
AT RANDOM ON THE FLOOR AND
WINDOWSILL – WORK WITH THE
BLACK SQUARES OF THE WINDOW.

the big picture

Large-scale paintings have become increasingly popular in recent years – thanks, perhaps, to the vogue for loft living. Most people equate loft spaces with big, modern abstracts, such as Jackson Pollock's paint-splattered canvases. Pop artist James Rosenquist covered entire walls with paintings such as *Area Code*, which comprised four canvases featuring brash blocks and squiggles of colour. But big does not necessarily mean abstract or modern. Huge old-fashioned portraits in ornate gilt frames hang on the walls behind the beds in the minimalist white rooms of the fashionable Paramount Hotel in New York, forming the perfect counterpoint to an otherwise stark modernity. This is an idea that could work equally well in either a loft or a minimal-style Georgian home. Hung floor-to-ceiling, big pictures also work very effectively in small spaces.

ABOVE: A FLOOR-TO-CEILING IMAGE WORKS WELL IN A SMALL SPACE. HERE, A MURAL HAS BEEN PAINTED DIRECTLY ONTO THE WALL IN A HALLWAY.

RIGHT: USE A COLOURFUL ABSTRACT CANVAS TO CREATE AN IMPACT IN A NEUTRAL CREAM SETTING.

FAR RIGHT: THE POWER OF ONE: SOMETIMES A SOLITARY PAINTING CAN TRANSFORM SPACE DRAMATICALLY.

LEFT: STRENGTH IN NUMBERS –
A MULTITUDE OF SMALL DRAWINGS
GROUPED TOGETHER SYMMETRICALLY
GIVES A SENSE OF ORDER AND BALANCE.
IN THIS INSTANCE, THE RED, WHITE
AND BLACK COLOUR SCHEME ALSO
CREATES A HARMONIOUS COHERENCE.

small pictures, prints and photos

Small pictures – particularly antique
watercolours, for example, where the detail is
very fine – work best in small rooms, like a lobby
or lavatory. But it is also worth remembering that
there can be strength in numbers: a multitude of
framed black-and-white prints is strikingly
effective on a staircase or in a hallway, as is an
entire wall devoted to framed photographs or
prints. In order to give a sense of harmony and
continuity rather than one of random chaos,
however, it is best to display them all in the
same style of mount or frame.

Repetition can also be used to powerful
effect – the sum of the parts offering a greater
impact than the whole. You could create a huge
montage from dozens of smaller panels, or
simply display three small sketches by the same
artist. In a way, this arrangement echoes the
diptychs and triptychs that were produced from
the Middle Ages onwards. These devotional
paintings were made up of three painted
panels, hinged together so that the two outer
wings could be closed over the central panel.

ABOVE: A STAIRCASE IS THE IDEAL
PLACE TO HANG A SERIES OF PICTURES –
IN THIS CASE, SMALL, COLOURFUL
ARTWORKS IN BOX-STYLE FRAMES.

LEFT: A CLUSTER OF SMALL PHOTOS
LOOKS NEAT AND CONTAINED ON
THREE COMPACT WHITE SHELVES.

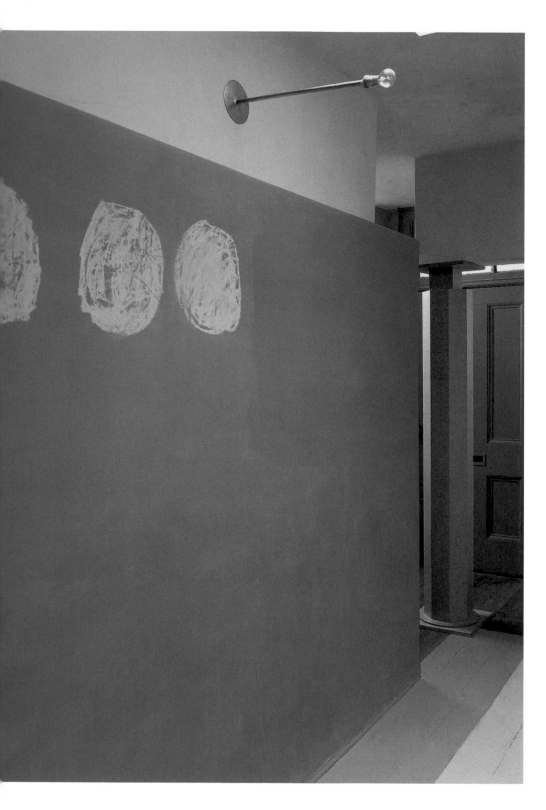

paint your own canvas

If you cannot afford to buy the right picture for
your flat, or can't find one you like, why not paint
something yourself? If you pine for a Damien
Hirst *Spot* painting (which start at £20,000),
you could paint your own – with the help of
a compass (to draw the spots) and some brightly
coloured household gloss paint. If you want
a large canvas featuring big blocks or swirls of
colour – to fill a loft space, for example – do-it-
yourself painting can be particularly rewarding.
The big advantage of painting your own canvas
is that you can create something that is exactly
the right size and colour for your space. You will
need to buy a few brushes, a canvas (or some
good-quality paper) in addition to a pot or two
of standard household gloss paint – as used by
Gary Hume and Damien Hirst. You could even
reproduce a Damien Hirst *Spin* painting: just
drop paint onto a spinning canvas in order to
get random but colourful results. Alternatively,
you could adopt the technique used by Matisse
for large-scale works such as *The Snail*, cutting
and tearing shapes from painted paper and
sticking them onto a canvas.

ABOVE: THE ADVANTAGE OF PAINTING
YOUR OWN CANVAS IS THAT YOU CAN
CREATE AN ARTWORK TO COMPLEMENT
THE COLOUR SCHEME OF YOUR LIVING
SPACE FOR A PERFECT MATCH.

OTHER FORMS OF WALL ART

wall paintings/murals

Instead of viewing art as something that comes neatly packaged in a frame, try to picture your walls as giant canvases. After all, artists in Renaissance Italy painted directly onto wet plaster to create magnificent frescoes. Nobody is suggesting that you recreate Michelangelo's Sistine Chapel ceiling, but it is easy to daub walls with bright swirls of colour – as modern artists such as Jacques-Henri Lartigue and Julian Schnabel have done in their homes. Unless you are a skilled artist, it is best to choose something simple and two-dimensional rather than aiming for depth and perspective. But you could also base a mural on a picture or photograph and scale up the image to fit the wall by using a grid. Or you could employ the services of a professional painter to do it for you.

BELOW LEFT: PAINTING DIRECTLY ONTO WALLS IS PARTICULARLY EASY IF YOU OPT FOR ROBERT INDIANA-STYLE WORD ART.

BELOW RIGHT: GRAFFITI SCRAWLS OR FREESTYLE CARICATURES – THERE ARE NO RULES WHEN IT COMES TO TREATING A WALL AS A BLANK CANVAS.

RIGHT: MAKE A STATEMENT WITH WALL SCRAWLS AND A BLOWN-UP BLACK-AND-WHITE PHOTOGRAPH.

BELOW RIGHT: WORDS PASTED ONTO BOARDS AND PROPPED AROUND THE HOUSE MAKE MORE THAN A VISUAL STATEMENT. ARTIST TRACEY EMIN HAS MADE USE OF WORD ART WITH A BRILLIANT NEON SIGN WHICH READS: 'FANTASTIC TO FEEL BEAUTIFUL AGAIN'.

Transforming your wall into a striking canvas need not involve paint at all. Instead, you could highlight textural finishes, using different wood veneers to create a chequerboard pattern on one surface. Alternatively, try combining screen-printed paper panels with a bold paint, or use ready-made wallpaper panels, which are an excellent way to create a colourful patchwork display. Simply attach them to the wall using Velcro pads, removable sticky pads, or double-sided adhesive tape.

Photocopies offer another innovative way to cover an expanse of wall. Simply choose a black-and-white photograph, or even an image from a book, get it blown up at a photocopy shop and then paste it onto the wall. Or take lots of smaller copies of the same image and paste them in a repetitive pattern over a large area.

If one had to nominate the twenty-first-century version of the painted canvas, however, it would be the hologram projection. Ian Schrager's fashionable St Martin's Lane hotel in London projects images of a shark at the entrance to the bar, for example. The scope is huge. All you need to fill a room with larger-than-life images is a projector and your favourite image or photograph captured on transparency. You could project stylish black-and-white images in your bedroom, or relaxing pictures of tropical beaches and sunsets in your living areas. Moreover, because these images are transient, you can change the look or mood of a room in an instant.

HOW TO MAKE YOUR OWN MURAL OR WALL PAINTING

To paint directly onto walls you need to first prepare them:
- Decrepit plaster needs to be resurfaced.
- Paint will not adhere to a surface if it is dirty, grimy or greasy, so start by washing down the wall with a sugar soap solution.
- Begin by painting the walls a base colour. Quick-drying paint is best when more than one colour is to be applied.
- To paint the actual picture, use thinned acrylic over a wall painted with ordinary emulsion. You can also paint your mural in poster paint, thinned oil-based paints, signwriter's paint or emulsion.

pinboards

Who says that only serious artwork merits a place on the wall? A simple pinboard featuring postcards, photos or children's drawings makes a very personal piece of art. It was Kurt Schwitters, an artist working in the 1920s, who first introduced this concept of art. He was particularly fond of 'found' objects – from bus tickets and bits of linoleum to worn-out shoe soles – which he used to create collages and fragmented

arrangements. Schwitter's collages did not involve a paintbrush or canvas but the end result was still powerful.

There are many different contemporary ways to develop Schwitters's original idea. You could, for example, make a montage of mementos from foreign trips as a visual reminder of your travels, or run a single line of postcards along a wall or around a room. You could even decorate an entire wall of the lavatory with a collage. Another idea is to update a postcard collage to reflect the seasons, using pictures of blue skies and tropical waters in the summer and leafy New England scenes in the autumn. The ultimate personal collage, however, is one that is made up of photos of your friends. The appeal of pinboard art is that it usually offers fascinating insights into the owner's personality and lifestyle. Put simply, it is the art of (real) life.

ABOVE: A PINBOARD DISPLAY CAN BE
VERY PERSONAL. THIS ONE BELONGS
TO TEXTILE DESIGNER CATH KIDSTON.

RIGHT: A KURT SCHWITTERS-STYLE
ASSEMBLAGE OF OBJECTS.

TOP RIGHT: DESIGNER CAROLYN
QUARTERMAINE'S THREE-DIMENSIONAL
PINBOARD AND WORK SPACE.

FAR RIGHT: A GIANT COLLAGE
OF POSTCARDS MAKES FOR
A COLOURFUL WORK OF ART.

blackboard art

Through the centuries many artists have harnessed the written word in the name of creativity. The impact is created not just by the word itself but also by the use of colour and graphic design. Roy Lichtenstein's oil on canvas featuring the word ART, picked out in red and white on a brash yellow background, is a good example of the genre; so, too are Tracey Emin's childish scrawl paintings. She has also sewn names, words and text onto fabrics and cushions, and created a neon blue sign, which reads 'Fantastic To Feel Beautiful Again' – quite literally the last word in art.

Even something as mundane as a grocery list or a message scrawled across a blackboard on a kitchen wall can be viewed as art.

The idea was originally developed by Jean-Michel Basquiat, an American painter, who started out using magic markers to create graffiti on the walls of buildings. By the early 1980s he had become famous for his crayon-and-paint drawings, featuring scrawled messages and texts on unprimed canvas. It is an idea that many modernists have incorporated into their homes, including Ilse Crawford, former editor of *Elle Decoration* magazine. Contemporary architect Vincent Van Duysen is also a fan of art scribbles, devoting one wall of his kitchen to a blackboard for scrawling messages. With so much technology around, the beauty of blackboard art lies in its childlike simplicity.

LEFT: BLACKBOARD ART WAS PIONEERED BY ARTIST JEAN-MICHEL BASQUIAT.

ABOVE: EVEN A SHOPPING LIST HAS ARTISTIC MERIT. A WHOLE WALL IN THE HOME OF ARCHITECT VINCENT VAN DUYSEN IS GIVEN OVER TO A BLACKBOARD.

wallpaper

Love it or loathe it, wallpaper still provides the background art in most people's homes. In recent years it has been frowned upon by the style police, who favour pristine white walls instead. But wallpaper is swinging back into fashion, as ultra-hip interiors magazine, *Wallpaper* illustrates. The fact that artist Damien Hirst has also turned his talents to this medium, designing silver paper covered with a multi-coloured pill motif for his London restaurant Pharmacy, serves to further underline the trend.

The latest wallpaper designs are very different from the tightly repeated patterns that covered the walls of the sitting rooms in our grandparents homes. Featuring large-scale motifs, chinoiserie florals and modern geometrics, they are works of art in their own right, with prices of up to £130 per roll to match.

Images produced by artists are being transferred to the medium of wallpaper; in Tracy Kendall's case, single-stem flowers, and knives, forks and spoons. At the same time a new crop of wallpaper designers, such as Neisha Crossland and Ottilie Stevenson, could easily be described as artists. Many of them take the richness of fabric designs as their inspiration. Starting out as a textile designer, Neisha Crossland uses motifs from silk kimonos and flower prints as the basis for her patterns, while Ottilie Stevenson's chinoiserie collection was inspired by a swatch of silk found in a Parisian flea market. Jane Gordon Clark, meanwhile, has used her background in art history and her training as a painter to develop her hand-printed papers, because, she says, 'It's like clothing a wall with a richness you cannot achieve with paint. The difference between handmade and commercial prints is like comparing haute couture to the ready-to-wear.'

Hung as banners, or pasted on to walls in groups of two or three, the latest wallpaper images are larger than life and turn the concept of all-over wall patterning on its head. Jocelyn Warner's *Larger Than Life* wallpaper collection, for example, reproduces

TOP: A SINGLE STRIP OF WALLPAPER BY TRACY KENDALL LOOKS BEAUTIFUL HUNG AS A BANNER ON A PLAIN WHITE WALL.

LEFT: A FAVOURITE PIECE OF WALLPAPER PASTED TO A BOARD MAKES FOR AN INTERESTING ARTWORK. SIMPLY PROP IT UP AGAINST A WALL.

ABOVE: AN INNOVATIVE TAKE ON
RETRO-STYLE, GEOMETRICALLY-
PATTERNED WALLPAPER.

ABOVE RIGHT: NEISHA CROSSLAND'S
ARTISTIC DESIGNS OFFER A MODERN
SPIN ON TRADITIONAL PATTERNS.

RIGHT: USE WALLPAPER WITH THE FLAIR
AND VISUAL SENSE OF AN ARTIST IN
ORDER TO MAKE A TONE-ON-TONE
COLOUR STATEMENT.

'When a budget cannot stretch to pictures and paintings, wallpaper can add instant glamour.' Ottilie Stevenson, wallpaper designer, who began her career with Osborne & Little.

images from nature in bold, screen-printed papers. The effect is of a one-off mural; hang it either on one wall or in single strips with painted walls as a complementary background.

Although large-scale designs are best in large rooms, you can use wallpaper in many inventive ways. The very brave hang clashing panels of wallpaper or create a patchwork pattern of different designs. Alternatively, you could hang it in horizontal or vertical panels across the room. If you opt for a horizontal panel, try picking out a colour or tone from the pattern to paint the wall below it. Or vice versa. You can also create striking optical effects using different kinds of striped wallpapers. Moreover, if you are attracted to a particular wallpaper pattern but do not want to cover your walls with it, you can simply frame a small piece and hang it above the mantelpiece.

The first versions of wallpaper can be traced back to the medieval Dukes of Burgundy, who hung silk banners, especially cut to fit around doorways and windows, on the bare stone walls of their castles. In the late nineteenth century William Morris – who believed that decoration was the beginning of art – created some of the most distinctive and well-known wallpapers of our time. His intricate patterns of lush flora and fauna fostered the English fascination for 'all-over' patterns. Morris's peacocks and pomegranates, acanthus leaves and chrysanthemums were pasted not just on walls, but on ceilings, too, and created a rich and elaborate effect throughout the home.

Since Morris's time wallpapers have, more than any other furnishing feature, defined the eras in which they were designed. They also make definite statements about the style of a dwelling and its owner. From the pretty Laura Ashley florals of country cottages to the psychedelic patterns that emerged in the 1960s and the disco-mirror papers of the late 1970s, wallpaper is the most proletarian of art forms. However, whether you choose to paper the walls with old editions of the *Financial Times* or gild your bedroom with pages of gold leaf, wallpaper is a versatile medium and should be exploited to its full artistic potential.

ABOVE: CREATE AN ARTISTIC WALL FEATURE USING SINGLE STRIPS OF CONTRASTING WALLPAPER FOR AN INNOVATIVE COLLAGE.

step on it; drape it

'in art as in love, instinct is enough'

ANATOLE FRANCE

FLOOR COUTURE

carpets and rugs

A striking rug or carpet can make as much of an impact in the modern home as a painting or sculpture – especially on fashionable bare floorboards or against a natural floor-covering. Floor-level art is one of the best ways to embellish your surroundings, whether you choose a custom-made design by a well-known rug-maker such as Christopher Farr, or a colourful patchwork of cheap clashing kilims. Think of your floor as an empty canvas, and use rugs and kilims to make bold statements as well as break up space. There are many possibilities: a pale- or pastel-coloured *dhurrie* on a dark wood floor; a vibrant rug in a glossy, black marble bathroom or a pretty Portuguese floral rug in an otherwise austere room. Choose your carpet carefully and it can have as much appeal as a colourful Picasso poster on a plain white wall. Moreover, the beauty of rugs is their versatility. They do not lock you into a permanent arrangement. Instead they can be moved around or rolled away – the ultimate in portable and unpretentious art.

ABOVE: THESE RUGS FEATURING
GEOMETRIC OP-ART DESIGNS BY
CHRISTINE VAN DER HURD ARE
WORKS OF ART IN THEIR OWN RIGHT.

RIGHT: ANOTHER EXAMPLE OF
CHRISTINE VAN DER HURD'S
EXUBERANT FLOOR COVERINGS.

LEFT: A PATCHWORK RUG ON BARE
FLOORBOARDS NOT ONLY BREAKS UP
SPACE, BUT HAS THE SAME EFFECT AS
A PAINTING ON AN EMPTY WALL.

LEFT: THIS CUSHION AND RUG MAKE A POWERFUL IMPACT ON THEIR SURROUNDINGS, CREATING AN ALMOST THREE-DIMENSIONAL OP-ART EFFECT.

BELOW RIGHT: RUGS AND CUSHIONS ARE NOT PERMANENT SO YOU CAN AFFORD TO BE BOLD WHEN INTRODUCING THEM INTO YOUR HOME.

'There is a beautiful midnight blue Chinese rug on the floor of my library that I inherited from my grandmother and I've painted the room to match.'

Kathleen Turner, actress.

items, carpets belong on the floor. Nevertheless, it is best to avoid putting an expensive rug in an area of heavy traffic such as an entrance hall.

It makes as much sense to decorate a room around a favourite rug as it does a painting. The alternative is to commission a carpet that complements your decor. But where do you place a carpet for maximum impact? Placing a rug between two facing sofas or in front of a fireplace, are traditional arrangements, although more random groupings can be equally successful in less conventional surroundings. A good example is the antique Turkish carpets and kilims that are displayed in a random patchwork on the floor of designer Soledad Twombly's studio in Italy. The resulting bohemian mix of texture, colour and pattern is the perfect counterpoint to the studio's modern whitewashed brick walls and high ceilings.

A brightly patterned rug is the perfect foil to a cream room and helps to soften the architectural lines of modern decor. Often the *style du jour* is dictated by the tastes of interior decorators. An example is the recent trend for nineteenth-century Aubusson carpets among New York's elite, whereby no Upper East Side apartment was considered complete without one.

Oriental carpets, kilims and modern rugs have always enjoyed fine-art status, partly perhaps because of their long life span. Even a delicate silk carpet will outlive its owner by several hundred years – while good-quality carpets improve with age, which is why they are so eminently collectable.

Many twentieth-century rugs have also become collector's items, including the psychedelic floor coverings made by fashion designer Emilio Pucci in the 1960s. Meanwhile, the abstract rugs made by designer Eileen Gray look as modern today as they did in the 1920s. More recently, the colourful designs of Christopher Farr's hand-knotted rugs have become synonymous with loft living. As well as creating his own designs, Farr has also commissioned rugs by Rifat Ozbek, Georgina Von Etzdorf and Romeo Gigli. New York-based designer Christine Van Der Hurd, meanwhile, has been nicknamed 'the queen of rugs'. Her bold stripes and geometric shapes are cut deep into the pile to create patterns in relief. Other designers include Tracy Hillier, whose fin-shaped rugs incorporate blocks of colour – as well as designs that feature brushed aluminium inserts – and Annette Nix, who includes sheet metal, Perspex and chain mail into her work.

Even though many contemporary rugs are considered works of art, they are also durable enough to withstand a lifetime underfoot. Some people like to hang expensive carpets on the wall – a practice that dates back several centuries. Until the advent of machine weaving, carpets were the preserve of a small, wealthy sector of society – and until the nineteenth century, they were draped on tables or hung on walls, but never laid on the floor. Today, this practice seems slightly ludicrous. Unless they are antique collector's

TIPS FOR SERIOUS CARPET BUYERS

- Study the subject and learn how to tell the difference between carpets.
- Insist that the dealer provides evidence of a rug's provenance if it is valuable or antique – good dealers will do this automatically.
- Buy at auction or from a specialist dealer and never from a carpet shop that boasts a so-called 'closing down' sale.
- It is fairly easy to recognize a good-quality carpet: the colours and lustre will be rich, and it will have a dense pattern and weave.

TIPS ON CARING FOR CARPETS AND RUGS

- If a good-quality rug is going on bare boards, it will need underlay to prevent people from slipping and also to protect the underside of the rug from wear. Secure the underlay on hard-wood surfaces with special bonding strips bought from department stores.
- If you spill wine (or any other liquid) on a carpet, tackle it immediately. Blot the spillage with a paper towel or damp cloth to remove as much as possible before the liquid has a chance to sink into the pile. Then wash gently with detergent, working from the outside rim to the centre.
- Do not scrub or use salt on a stain as this may damage the fibres.
- If you spill grease or fat on a carpet, blot it immediately, wait until it is dry, and then clean the stain with drycleaning fluid.
- If your carpet or rug is pale, it may be worth considering a stain-inhibition treatment.

TIPS FOR CHOOSING FLOOR COUTURE

- Use decorative patterns to enliven dull surfaces or empty spaces: the intense colours of a fine oriental rug can add richness to an otherwise austere hallway, for example.
- Do not be afraid to look to other cultures in your search for the perfect rug: ethnic weaves add warmth and texture, and sit well in contemporary interiors.
- Choose a pattern for the impact that it will have in its intended home, not just because you like the colour blend or design.
- Do not be afraid to mix ethnic carpets and textiles from different cultures: a Navajo blanket draped over a sofa will combine easily with a range of Turkish rugs on the floor.
- Remember that rugs come in a wide range of shapes and sizes; they are not just rectangular or square. Contemporary carpet-makers such as Tracy Hillier, for example, are creating unusual morphic and flowing shapes. So think about what shape is going to work best in your space.

tiles and mosaics

Mosaic is floor art *par excellence*. The practice of covering floors with small pieces of tile or *tesserae*, laid in mortar and arranged in decorative or geometric designs, dates back to the Roman Empire. The appeal of a mosaic lies in the intricacy and intense colours of the design. However, because it is very labour-intensive (not to mention expensive to lay), mosaic is best used in smaller rooms. Moreover, while simple mosaics involving geometric patterning can be carried out by an amateur, more complicated pictorial designs require the skills of a professional.

HOW TO INSTALL A MOSAIC FLOOR

There are two ways to create a mosaic floor:
- The first involves sticking individual pieces onto the floor one by one. This is really only suitable for small areas.
- The second method is to build up the floor in sections. You first stick the mosaic pieces, finished surface face down, to paper using water-soluble glue. The back of the mosaic is then grouted and the mosaic pressed, right side (and paper) up, onto the floor. Then wet the paper to dissolve the glue and peel it away.

Using hard tiles is less labour-intensive, which makes them a practical and attractive alternative. Available in a range of rainbow colours, and a variety of textures and sizes, ceramic tiles can be used to create bold patterns or contrasting borders. Indeed, they offer unlimited artistic scope. Because they are regular in dimension and colouring, they produce a sharp, contemporary look. Tiled floors are hard-wearing and therefore particularly suited to kitchens, bathrooms and hallways.

ABOVE: THE APPEAL OF A TILED
FLOOR LIES IN THE INTRICACY AND
INTENSE COLOURS OF THE DESIGN.
IN THIS MOROCCAN-INSPIRED FLOOR,
PAINTED TILES ARE PLACED RANDOMLY
AND ACT AS MINIATURE WORKS OF ART.

LEFT: A COLOURFUL, MODERN
PATCHWORK-EFFECT FLOOR.

RIGHT: WHATEVER YOUR TASTES,
YOU CAN CREATE A BIG IMPACT
WITH A TILED FLOOR. BUT IF YOU
OPT FOR AN ALL-OVER PATTERN, IT IS
BEST TO KEEP YOUR FURNITURE SIMPLE.

TEXTILES

Textile design has never been accorded the same artistic recognition as painting or furniture design. Textiles do count as works of art, however, and can be used in the form of soft furnishings; you could even frame a piece of cloth and then hang it on the wall. While there is something a bit dubious about printing Monet's poppies onto a duvet cover – the perfect example of how not to incorporate 'old' art in the modern world – there are many contemporary and antique textile prints which are recognized as an art form.

Ever since the 1940s and 1950s, when Czech-born textile designers Zika and Lida Ascher commissioned artists such as Henri Matisse, Jean Cocteau and Henry Moore to create designs for a series of scarves, the line between textile designer and artist has blurred. Sonia Delaunay, for example, worked as a painter and textile designer simultaneously. Delaunay, whose decorative geometric designs were the height of fashion in the 1920s, regarded textile and commercial design as an extension of painting, and was a major exponent of the fusion between art and fashion. She even produced a series of curtains using her own art fabric, and incorporated bright colours and pieces of text.

If you want to lend your textiles a fine-art status, the trick is to remember that they do not have to fulfil their original design function: use a patchwork quilt as a tablecloth, for example, or a bedspread or antique shawl as a wall hanging, or suspend a sheer white Indian wedding sari as a curtain. You could even display an antique quilt on the wall above a bed. Textiles are not permanent, so you can afford to be bold when you introduce them into your home.

carolyn quartermaine: textile artist extraordinaire

One of the most influential textile designers working today is Carolyn Quartermaine. Her delectable hand-painted textiles – often covered in gold copperplate script – can be used as curtains, wall hangings, cushions or upholstery. She treats an entire room as an artist might use a canvas: delicate fabrics flung across a table – apparently at random – create the impression of a beautiful still-life, while brightly coloured silks in shades of green, lemon, pink and lilac serve as wall hangings or are suspended from the ceiling like an ethereal art installation. She also produces fabric and paper collages and has transferred her textile art designs onto upholstery, breathing new life into an antique salon chair, for example.

LEFT: BEAUTIFUL TEXTILES CAN BE INTRODUCED INTO THE HOME IN MANY WAYS – IN THIS CASE WITH A STACK OF NOTEBOOKS COVERED WITH FABRIC.

ABOVE: USE ORNATE FABRICS TO INJECT A SHARP SHOT OF COLOUR INTO A ROOM.

LEFT: TEXTILE ARTIST CAROLYN
QUARTERMAINE BALANCES THE
ORNATENESS OF AN ANTIQUE FRENCH
CHAIR WITH THE SIMPLICITY OF HER
HAND-PAINTED SILK FABRIC.

RIGHT: CAROLYN QUARTERMAINE
USES AN ENTIRE ROOM IN HER
HOUSE-CUM-SHOWROOM AS AN
ARTIST MIGHT USE A CANVAS. THE
END RESULT IS A COMPOSITION
THAT IS VISUALLY PLEASING.

'The basis of all that
I do is art and my
home is my studio.'

Carolyn Quartermaine, textile artist.

'The basis of all that I do is art,' says
Carolyn Quartermaine. Indeed, in her hands,
even the humble cushion is treated as a
painting, and edged with contrasting piping.

Her beautiful effects are created in several
ways: she applies emulsion paint onto silk using
her hand or wide brushstrokes; drops textile paint
onto wet fabrics; and hand-paints directly onto
upholstery, daubing a dusty pink rose onto the
back of a gilded antique chair, for example.

antique shawls and modern throws

Beautiful antique and modern shawls alike can be draped over chairs, sofas and beds as a form of art within the home. The rule is that a little goes a very long way: one shawl used as a flash of colour and richness in an otherwise light, minimal room looks great. Use too many, however, and the effect can be drab and Victorian rather than contemporary. The appeal of antique shawls and fabrics lies in their exotic designs and rich, jewel-like colours; an antique throw, framed and hung on a wall or tossed over a side table, can reinvent a room; while a classic paisley shawl or fabric printed with a bold pattern or rich colours can also create a focal point.

The Kashmir or Indienne shawl – first imported into Europe in the 1760s – was the predecessor of the modern pashmina. Made popular by Horatio Nelson's Lady Hamilton, these exotic wraps were as much a measure of social standing as an indicator of style.

Obviously, the cost of an antique shawl depends on its age and state of repair, but the quality of the weaving also plays a part. When you are attempting to date a shawl, remember that early nineteenth-century European designs are long, narrow and decorated at each end. Colour is also a giveaway: earlier shawls are characterized by natural colours (synthetic dyes allowed shawls to be produced in brighter shades after 1850).

As a general rule, the more intricate the pattern and the greater the number and depth of colours used to make up the design, the better the quality of the shawl. Most common are mass-produced shawls from Paisley, which start at around £40; vintage shawls, on the other hand, start at about £2,500, while an outstanding piece of work by a French designer could cost £10,000 plus.

LEFT: A MODERN THROW CAN ADD
TEXTURE AND VISUAL INTEREST TO
AN OTHERWISE PLAIN SOFA.

RIGHT: REINVENT A ROOM BY
DRAPING COLOURFUL SHAWLS
OVER PIECES OF FURNITURE.

FAR RIGHT (TOP AND BOTTOM):
LAVISHLY EMBROIDERED SHAWLS
ARE THROWN OVER THE SOFAS IN
THE HOME OF NEW YORK BOUTIQUE
OWNER, LAURIE MCLENDON.

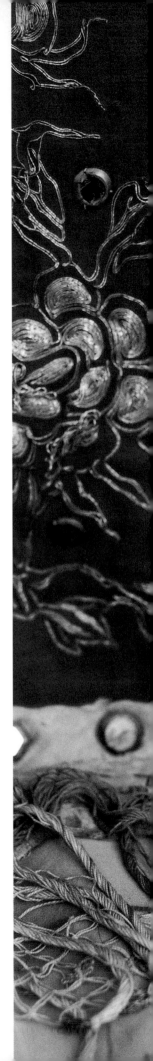

wall hangings

The term 'wall hanging' tends to conjure up images of fusty old medieval tapestries depicting scenes of long-forgotten battles. But modern versions have little in common with the ornate, embroidered hangings that were considered status symbols centuries ago. Sian Tucker's colourful organza wall hangings are as contemporary as a piece of Conran furniture. They feature graphic designs and layer sheer over opaque fabrics to give an extra dimension.

In medieval Europe tapestries and textiles were popular not only for their decorative qualities but also because they acted as

barriers against draughts and helped provide some insulation, however meagre, against the cold. The nobility, who were always on the move, lavished their money on portable hangings. As the Middle Ages progressed, an increasing number of sumptuous wall hangings were produced, using Florentine velvets or fine silks from Venice. In late seventeenth-century England, it became the fashion to cover entire walls with decorative fixed hangings – not just tapestries but lighter woven damasks and watered silks – which were the precursors of wallpaper.

If you want to create a modern wall hanging, you will find there is plenty of scope. A framed silk scarf, or a series of framed fabric pieces can look very striking. You can also try framing strips of fabrics cut into unusual shapes – long and thin, for example, to fit narrow walls for an interesting effect. Some textiles can be difficult to frame but old and delicate fabrics should always be mounted behind glass or Plexiglass to protect them from sunlight and dust. If the fabric is inexpensive, however, you could simply hang a piece on a wall or above a fireplace. Another idea – and a creative way to divide up an open-plan room – is to hang a tapestry or fabric from a rod that has been suspended from the ceiling.

ABOVE: ANOTHER IDEA IS TO HANG A PIECE OF YOUR FAVOURITE FABRIC FROM A ROD OR RAIL ON THE WALL. HERE, CATH KIDSTON HAS HUNG ONE OF HER OWN VINTAGE-INSPIRED FLORAL FABRICS FROM A TOWEL RAIL.

LEFT: A MODERN TAKE ON THE WALL HANGING BY SIAN TUCKER, WHO USES COLOURFUL FABRICS IN AN ARTISTIC WAY.

RIGHT: TOO GOOD TO PUT ON THE FLOOR, THIS RUG BY CHRISTINE VAN DER HURD MAKES A FABULOUS OP ART-STYLE WALL HANGING. ITS COLOURS PICK UP THE WARM GOLDEN TONES OF THE FLOORBOARDS AND THE TAUPE OF THE SWIVEL CHAIR.

out of the closet: the art of clothing

It is becoming increasingly popular to display clothing as domestic art. There is no reason why you cannot give your favourite pieces a starring role in your home – framing a favourite scarf, floating a chiffon dress on a hanger in front of a window, or suspending a tiny pink tutu from the ceiling with a pink ribbon. After all, kimonos have been collected and displayed on walls for centuries. It is likely that you have a treasure trove of artistic possibilities stashed in your wardrobe – even a dress hanging from a door or antique hat stand can become a spontaneous still-life.

But can clothing really be considered as art? It is a debate that has raged since Elsa Schiaparelli flirted with Surrealist imagery in the 1930s, collaborating with Salvador Dali on a trompe-l'oeil tea dress. In her autobiography, *Shocking Life*, she wrote: 'Dress designing is to me not a profession but an art.' Other designers who have been inspired by art include Yves Saint-Laurent, whose 1965 Mondrian dress was an imitation

of the bright blocks of red, yellow and blue used by the Dutch abstract painter, offering a perfect example of a piece of clothing which could also be framed and used as an artwork. Saint-Laurent has also paid tribute to Picasso in the design of some of his elaborately beaded couture gowns. Too beautiful to be kept hidden in a closet, these are masterpieces in their own right.

At the same time there is a new clique of designers creating clothes which blur the boundaries between apparel and art. Working to commission, Heather Belcher makes monochrome felt walls around a sartorial theme, with titles such as *Dress* or *Shirt*; Yayoi Kusama's golden evening bag encrusted with pasta, meanwhile, has been on display at the Serpentine Gallery in London. Emily Bates's dresses made of human hair and Hussein Chalayan's fibreglass frock have also explored the relationship between art and fashion.

ABOVE LEFT: THIS YVES SAINT-LAURENT DRESS, BASED ON A GEOMETRIC PAINTING BY PIET MONDRIAN, IS A GOOD EXAMPLE OF FASHION FUSED WITH ART.

FAR LEFT: USE YOUR FAVOURITE FASHION ACCESSORIES TO CREATE A TEMPORARY STILL-LIFE, RATHER THAN HIDING THEM IN A CUPBOARD.

ABOVE: A TRANSPARENT DRESS BY ALEXANDER MCQUEEN IS TRANSFORMED INTO AN ETHEREAL ARTWORK, HUNG FROM AN ANTIQUE GILT FRAME IN CAROLYN QUARTERMAINE'S HOME.

a window on art: curtains and blinds

RIGHT: A CREATIVE WAY TO DIVIDE UP AN
OPEN-PLAN SPACE IS TO HANG A PIECE
OF BEAUTIFUL FABRIC FROM A ROD
SUSPENDED FROM THE CEILING, AS SEEN
IN CAROLYN QUARTERMAINE'S BEDROOM.

BELOW: A VIVID PINK SILK-ORGANZA
SARI HUNG IN THE WINDOW OF CAROLYN
QUARTERMAINE'S HOME MAKES AN EYE-
CATCHING, PURELY DECORATIVE FEATURE.

BELOW RIGHT: PAINTING DIRECTLY
ONTO A ROLLER BLIND TURNS A
WINDOW INTO A WORK OF ART.

Curtains can be the most eye-catching feature in a room. The artist David Hockney was apparently fascinated by the fact that a curtain is just like a painting and that you can hang a curtain just as you would a picture. However, it's a fair bet that Hockney wasn't referring to the flowery chintz variety of drapes. These have little place in the modern home. Consider instead the bright multi-coloured spot-print curtains – made from a Vivienne Westwood fabric – that hang in the home of Jo Corré, owner of London lingerie shop Agent Provocateur. They are as much of an exclamation mark as one of Damien Hirst's *Spot* paintings. There is also something very humorous and fun about them.

You can create curtains that are works of art by using unusual materials such as flowing metal mesh or, in the case of interior designer, Orianna Fielding Banks, curtains made from blank CDs, which reflect the light and attract the eye. Similarly, computer

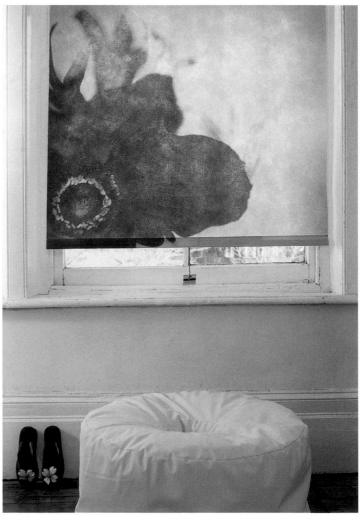

LEFT: CURTAINS MADE FROM MIRRORED
OR REFLECTIVE PANELS THAT CATCH THE
LIGHT ARE AN INNOVATIVE WAY TO
FRAME YOUR WINDOWS.

BELOW LEFT: EVEN A TRANSPARENT
SHOWER CURTAIN CAN BE TAKEN OUT
OF THE BATHROOM AND DRAPED
ARTISTICALLY ACROSS A ROOM.

RIGHT: A WINDOW PROVIDES A NATURAL
FRAME FOR A BOLD ARTISTIC STATEMENT
– IN THIS CASE, A POP ART-INSPIRED
PICTURE IMPRINTED ON A BEAD CURTAIN.

generated imagery can also create an almost three-dimensional effect with huge dramatic impact. Another option is to throw sheer fabrics over a pole and paint directly onto them using special fabric paints. Or try painting flower or leaf motifs onto a plain, white roller blind.

You do not need windows to hang curtains. A continuous curtain in an abstract pattern hung along one wall of a basement room, for example, gives the illusion of windows where there are none. You can even use sheer curtains as a flimsy room-divider to imbue your living space with an ethereal quality.

Windows – important architectural features in their own right – can also benefit from an artistic touch. Fashion designer Matthew Williamson, for example, created a colourful patchwork effect on the windows of a fashionable yoga centre in north London. The idea is easy to copy and you do not need stained glass to do it – just different coloured gel papers (the type used by photographers). Cut out squares of gel and paste them to the lower half of a window. In a light, white room the effect is particularly stunning.

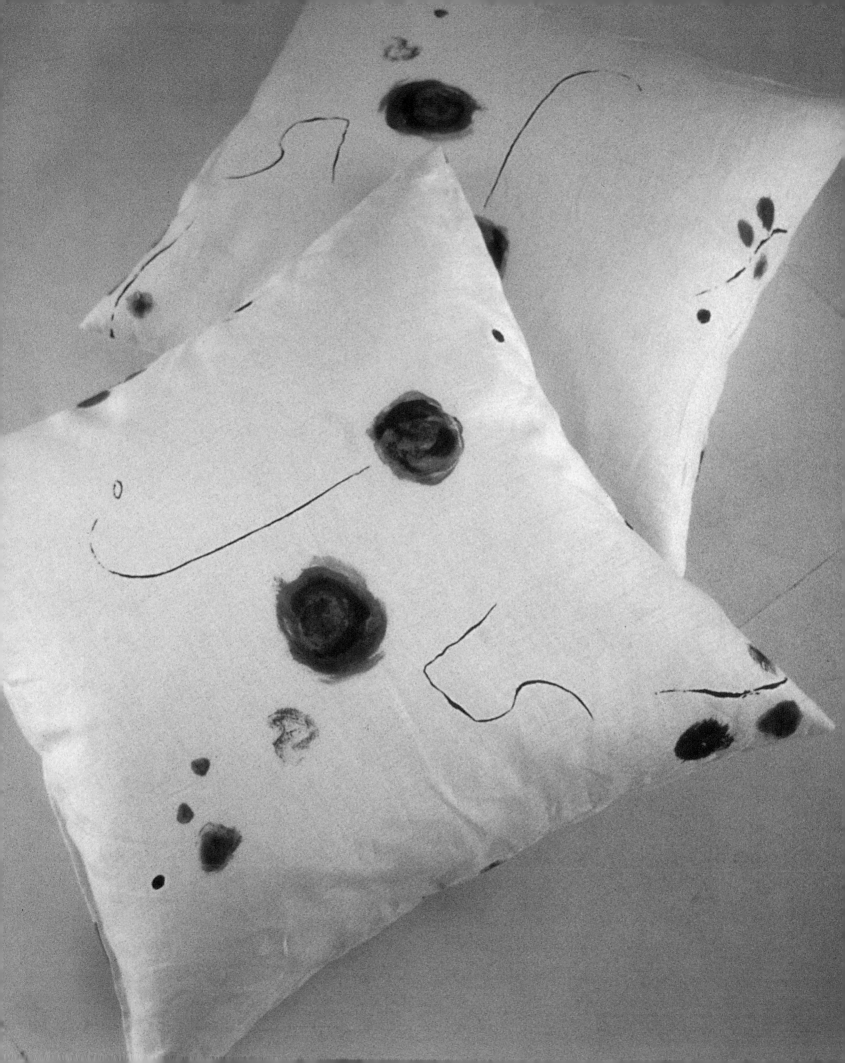

cushions

Not only have cushions become a 'must-have' fashion item in stylish homes but they also have artistic merit. Think of them as jewellery for a room – a small detail that can have a huge visual impact. Modern cushions are characterized by everything from Warhol-esque images of Chairman Mao to remnants of antique silk kimonos and sari fabrics, not to mention design company Wallace Sewell's creations, which feature rich patchwork and geometric patterns in bright colours. Emphasizing the relationship between the colours in a painting and the colours in your soft furnishings can also create a brilliant effect. Use cushions to pick up a shade you particularly like, or to create irreverent mixes of pattern. Either way, view them with an artist's eye.

FAR LEFT: THESE CUSHIONS ARE THE PERFECT EXAMPLE OF TEXTILE ART TRANSFERRED ONTO SOFT FURNISHINGS. THE PRINTED-LINEN COVERS ARE MADE FROM 'BLOSSOM' FABRIC, PART OF THE 'ORIENTAL SHADOWS' COLLECTION DESIGNED BY CAROLYN QUARTERMAINE FOR SAHCO HESSLEIN.

ABOVE LEFT: THINK OF CUSHIONS AS JEWELLERY FOR A ROOM, AND CHOOSE COLOURS AND PATTERNS CAREFULLY SO AS TO CREATE A BIG VISUAL IMPACT.

LEFT: STRIKING TEXTILES BY BRITISH DESIGNER CATH KIDSTON.

the collection

'there is something **tantalising** about bringing **objects** out into the **open** which are usually **hidden** away'

CAROLYN QUARTERMAINE,
ARTIST AND TEXTILE DESIGNER

'In my house in the country I'm a passionate collector of objects: old glass, insects – especially butterflies which were my hobby when I was young – and paintings.'

Sir Terence Conran.

RIGHT: COLLECT WHATEVER TAKES YOUR FANCY, BUT DISPLAY IT WITH CONVICTION, WHETHER IT IS A COLLECTION OF POSTERS, MUGS OR EMPTY JACK DANIELS' BOTTLES. THIS HOMEOWNER CLEARLY HAS A PASSION FOR THE POP ART ERA, AND ONE OF ITS MOST RECOGNIZABLE REPRESENTATIONS, THE CAMPBELL'S SOUP CAN; NOTE THE POP ART CONCEPT OF REPETITION.

THE URGE TO COLLECT

Many of us feel compelled to collect things from an early age: dolls, stamps, toy cars and teddy bears are typical examples. Teenagers use their collections to stake out their territory, covering their bedroom walls with posters of pop stars or sporting heroes. As adults we might progress to collecting prints, paintings, pottery or other artefacts. Even Terence Conran, the guru of uncluttered minimalist design, is an avid collector of assorted objects. I almost fell off the Conran sofa I was perched on when he declared during an interview: 'I am a passionate collector of objects: old glass, insects – especially butterflies which were my hobby when I was young – and paintings.'

Over the years, building up a collection becomes like a diary chronicling the events of your life. It is also an educational process and, over time, your tastes will become more discerning. Moreover, the process of acquiring, sorting and categorizing is all part of the pleasure of collecting.

You can really stamp your personality on a living space by displaying your favourite objects and collections, but bear in mind that a collection might also influence the ambience of a room: a display of Samurai swords or war memorabilia, for example, is unlikely to create a peaceful atmosphere in your sitting room, while huge numbers of toy cars or teddy bears in an adult's bedroom will make it resemble a playroom, and give the impression that the resident has not quite grown up.

Prints and paintings are two of the most obvious examples of collectable items. Glassware, silver and china are also popular. Those with esoteric tastes and a healthy bank account might collect anything from precious snuff boxes to Sèvres porcelain, but collecting need not be expensive. Nor do you need to make a collection of furniture, Fabergé eggs or other such rare objects from the past. You can collect anything that takes your fancy and that might mean fun rather than valuable items. The key is to trust your own taste, judgement and intuition. Anything – from collections of colourful teapots displayed on a plain white shelf to a multitude of snow domes or other kitsch miscellany – can have artistic merit if it is assimilated with energy and passion.

Collecting is subject to fashionable tastes and an area that has formerly been out of vogue can sometimes become popular again almost overnight. Ceramics, for example, used to be considered as dull as dishwater but recently they have become fashionable. Black-and-white photography has also become hip, with limited-edition prints of well-known photos starting at $10,000 plus. In addition, crafts, pop memorabilia and postcards have all joined the ranks of collectability, and are taken seriously enough to be traded at top auction houses. Always remember that the passage of time can transform mundane items into things of value; and today's junk could be tomorrow's object of desire.

period collecting

Serious collectors who like a particular artist or historical era often create focused collections based around their passion. British advertising guru Charles Saatchi has assembled a formidable collection of Brit Art, thanks to his adventurous tastes – and in a previous century, the Wallace family built up a collection of French eighteenth-century paintings and furniture, which was bequeathed to the British nation. Many American dynasties have also specialized in one era, allowing them to bequeath a collection of historical significance to a museum in their family name.

As collecting tastes are subject to trends, so too do historical periods go in and out of fashion. Art Nouveau, for example, with its large gaudy flowers and whiplash curves, was considered vaguely vulgar until its revival in the late 1950s and early 1960s. Similarly, the undervalued design work of the 1950s was rediscovered in the early 1980s. The same is true of certain artists. When American collectors Herbert and Ruth Schimmel began collecting Toulouse-Lautrec in the 1950s, for example, they had little competition and were able to build up an unrivalled collection of posters, drawings and letters. Similarly astute collectors invested in Picasso's late works in the 1970s, then regarded as inferior to his earlier works and available at a much lower price. Picasso's later artistic endeavours have since become better appreciated and consequently much more expensive.

Interestingly, contemporary art used to be relatively inexpensive in comparison to the art of the past. At one time, buying the work of a living artist was the natural thing to do if you did not have a lot of money to spend. Today, however, fledgling artists are very quickly hyped out of the reach of most people's pockets. Consequently, your money will often go further if you buy art from the past (see Collecting Paintings, page 98).

Many wealthy art collectors who have focused their attention on the paintings of a particular period like to show their collection against the authentic furniture and decor of that era. This means painstakingly reproducing paint colours and fabrics in the area in which you wish to show your collection, as Earl Spencer recently chose to do when he refurbished Althorp House, his family home in Northamptonshire, England, after rehanging the ancestral art collection. Stately homes aside, period furnishings can look static to the modern eye. Although the Wallace Collection, for example, is a superb example of its genre, Hertford House in London, where it is displayed, appears to have little relevance to contemporary living. Few of us possess an Old Master or a collection of eighteenth-century paintings, however, so the issue of period decor – and whether or not to invest in a sitting room full of gilded salon chairs – is not something that concerns us.

LEFT AND FAR LEFT: THE SETTINGS MAY
BE MODERN BUT SOME OF THE MOST
BEAUTIFUL OBJECTS IN THESE TWO
ROOMS ARE EIGHTEENTH CENTURY.

BELOW: FROM THE EAMES CHAIR TO
THE CONTEMPORARY CANVAS ON THE
WALL, EVERYTHING IN THIS ROOM IS
OF MODERNIST PERSUASION.

eclectic collecting

Some people have a magpie mentality and collect anything and everything, refusing to confine themselves to one type of object or single era. Distinguished nineteenth-century collector Sir John Soane adopted a boldly eclectic approach to collecting and assembled archaeological, architectural and aesthetic finds in his house in Lincoln's Inn Fields in London. Today, this approach would almost certainly be described as 'modern eclectic'. Eclectic is sometimes considered a derogatory term, meaning undisciplined or lacking in focus, but diversity can be attractive, while mixing periods and styles can give character to a living space. Modern art, for instance, mixes well with elegant eighteenth-century furniture. Artist Carolyn Quartermaine mixes furniture from different periods with flamboyance and flair – placing antique French salon chairs next to a 1940s trestle table, for example. There is, however, a fine line between giving your home quirky character and overwhelming it with a jumble of art and furnishings culled from different periods, cultures and media.

How, then, do you create a harmonious composition out of a hodgepodge of disparate objects? One of the most obvious ways is to create a sense of order by grouping things together in categories. A finely tuned eye can select disparate objects from different cultures

or eras and, by creating a relationship between textures and colours, place them confidently together. If you stick to a few artfully chosen pieces and keep the rest of the decor simple, you can get away with mixing furniture from different periods for an ultimately contemporary look. At the end of the day, the glue that holds a mixed collection together is the passion and personality of the person who created it.

LEFT TOP: A COLLECTION OF KITCHENWARE IS EFFECTIVELY 'FRAMED' ON OPEN SHELVES.

LEFT: A RESTRAINED DISPLAY OF DISPARATE OBJECTS EACH 'FRAMED' IN A WINDOW. THE SMALL SCALE ARTEFACTS

ARE, HOWEVER, DWARFED BY THE PROPORTIONS OF THE ROOM.

ABOVE: AN ECLECTIC COMBINATION OF PHOTOS, SCULPTURE, MODERN ART AND POP ART-INSPIRED CUSHIONS.

'There is only one reason to collect paintings – because you love the image and want to live with it forever.'

Antony Thorncroft, art critic.

when he was a student at London's Royal College of Art. It also means rigorously trawling the college degree shows for fresh talent (see pages 125 and 130). There is no doubt that those with a discerning eye can acquire bargains, and often the early works of an artist are the most interesting. As Samuel Butler once wrote, in *A Painter's Views on Painting*, 'The youth of an art is, like the youth of anything else – its most interesting period.'

Apart from the degree shows, the additional outlets for new and inexpensive art are fairs. Art fairs allow you to view the work of many artists in a short time, and you can often haggle over prices. Galleries can be intimidating to the novice collector; they are invariably empty of customers and staffed by disdainful assistants. You should be brave and visit the salerooms, too. Auctions can also be a great source of overlooked or currently unfashionable works. On a quiet day at Christie's you can pick up drawings and sketches by well-known names for as little as £150. Auctions can be dangerous, however, as it is easy to get carried away. The best option is to meet the artist in their studio, and look at their work before they are taken up by a gallery.

collecting paintings

Collecting paintings is considered the most pukka form of art investment. Most people buy one or two pictures purely as decoration, rather than attempting to build up a museum-quality collection. But buying art is curiously addictive and some people contract the bug after just a few purchases. According to art critic Antony Thorncroft, writing in the *Financial Times*, 'There is only one reason to collect paintings – because you love the image and want to live with it forever.' Having said that, there are people who make large sums of money from buying and selling art under the guise of collecting. Astute 'collectors' seek out the unfashionable, the undiscovered and the new, and then sell out at the height of movement's popularity, pocketing the profit and starting afresh in another overlooked area. This, however, is becoming increasingly difficult as fewer stones remain unturned.

The best option is to join the ranks of the collectors who try to buy the early works of unknown artists. To some extent, this is a question of being in the right place at the right time. Many people own paintings by David Hockney, which they picked up for a few pounds in the 1960s,

ABOVE LEFT: THE CURVY LINES OF THIS SKETCH CONTRAST WELL WITH THE ANGULAR SHAPE OF THE CHAIR.

TOP RIGHT: THESE RED CANVASES REALLY STAND OUT AGAINST CLASHING GREEN WALLS IN DANIELLE ARNAUD'S HOME. THE IMAGES, FROM LEFT TO RIGHT, ARE BY MARC HULSON AND INCLUDE: *LOFT*, (2000) ACRYLIC ON CANVAS; *HALF-LIGHT DIPTYCH*, (2000) OIL ON CANVAS; *FACES*, (2000) OIL ON CANVAS.

RIGHT: WORK WITH YOUR SPACE – HERE, A LARGE WALL RECESS IS THE PERFECT SPOT FOR THIS PHOTOGRAPH BY MARIE-FRANCE AND PATRICIA MARTIN: *APRES RICHTER, NU DESCENDANT* (1993/1998).

well-travelled: collecting regional art and artefacts

Because of the huge increase in travel to far-flung places, it has become fashionable to collect indigenous art. Increasingly, bringing back a souvenir from your holidays or travels means a painting, pot or woodcarving rather than the proverbial straw donkey. Mass-produced tourist tat apart, there are some fantastic finds in foreign countries. If you buy a painting of a local scene or some craftware made from materials that are indigenous to the area, it will act as a record of your travels and be all the more appealing for it. The best way to buy is to be prepared to venture off the beaten track in order to visit local

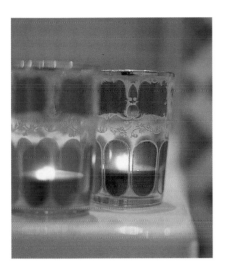

artists in their studios. The great advantage of regional art is that it is affordable. In many ways, people who buy art on their travels are simply following in the tradition of eighteenth-century scholars, who visited Greece and Rome on their Grand Tours, and brought back a mass of antiquities and artefacts to display in 'cabinets of curiosities' in their homes.

Some collectors choose to focus on the art of a particular region: masks, drums or carvings from Africa, for example, or aboriginal art from Australia. Most of us prefer to fill our homes with an assortment of 'finds' from all over the world. It is a great way of creating a totally individual collection. My own home contains an eclectic mix of objects which serve as testament to my travels as a fashion editor (and somehow, because I keep the rest of my surroundings simple, they all co-exist happily together). There are richly patterned silk carpets that I hiked up to a Turkish mountain village to buy; a cheerful watercolour painting of local fishermen bought from an artist's studio in the Seychelles; and colourful 'kikoi' fabrics picked up in a market in Tanzania. My favourite piece of all is an oil painting by a Vietnamese artist. When I saw it hanging in a gallery in Saigon I knew I had to have it. I was then forced to carry it around Vietnam rolled up in a rucksack for three weeks, but it was much more fun than buying something in the sterile environs of a London gallery.

'Every private collection formed by an individual in a lifetime is in a way a collection of souvenirs, a record of travel and discovery.'

Jacob Beam.

ABOVE AND ABOVE LEFT: FOREIGN COUNTRIES CAN BE A GOOD SOURCE OF INTERESTING ARTEFACTS SUCH AS THESE MOROCCAN-INSPIRED GLASSES AND CERAMICS.

FAR LEFT: SOUVENIRS FROM FOREIGN COUNTRIES CAN MAKE A STRIKING STILL-LIFE AS WELL AS A VISUAL RECORD OF YOUR TRAVELS. HERE, NEW YORK BOUTIQUE OWNER, LAURIE MCLENDON'S COLLECTION OF MATCHBOXES IS DISPLAYED ON A CHINESE BOOK.

kitsch collections

Although it may look less tasteful, displaying accumulated junk, trashy souvenirs and trivia is a humorous way to introduce kitsch and Pop Art into your home. Collections of shells in the bathroom, gaudy religious icons, toy cars, teddy bears or even tacky snow domes all come under this umbrella. Again, we can thank Pop Art for giving us a licence to like kitsch – and to collect all manner of knick-knacks and trivia. In the early years of Pop Art people began to fill their homes with the clutter of popular culture – souvenirs, advertising symbols and the imagery of packaging and mass media. The fact that museums were also acquiring this kind of art gave it a further seal of approval, prompting people to try and reproduce a similar style themselves. As Andy Warhol famously once said: 'Everyone is an artist.' Jasper Johns, for example, made two beer cans, whose design he liked, in painted bronze, elevating the everyday to the status of art. Conversely, at the same time, artists like Peter Blake, Andy Warhol and Richard Hamilton turned their talents to designing items such as record covers. Warhol, for example, designed record sleeves for Velvet Underground which, if you are lucky enough to possess one, could just as easily be framed and put on a wall. More recently, contemporary artists Tracey Emin and Damien Hirst have designed a limited-edition range of beer bottles for a well-known manufacturer.

LEFT: THE BRIGHT PACKAGING OF CHINESE FOODSTUFFS COMBINES WITH COLOURED GLASS TO CREATE A STRIKING DISPLAY.

RIGHT: THIS VIBRANT KITCHEN IS A SHRINE TO THE ART OF KITSCH.

You could even assemble a real-life interpretation of Andy Warhol's oil painting *Green Coca Cola Bottles* (1962) by making an artistic feature out of empty coke bottles. The point is

that class barriers have been well and truly broken down thanks to art, and high and low cultures have converged. It should also be remembered that some things – such as the fairy-light-covered shrines in some Buddhist temples – may be considered kitsch in one culture and sacred in another. Similarly, the curvilinear arabesque of Art Nouveau, once considered gaudy and kitsch, is now treated in collecting circles with as much reverence as the elaborate grace of eighteenth-century Rococo. You should feel free to surround yourself with exactly what you like – sometimes the brasher the better.

The Paris apartment of artists Pierre et Gilles offers one of the most exaggerated examples of kitsch in a domestic setting. Every available surface is decorated with plastic dolls, postcards, good-luck charms and silk flowers, displaying a joyful disregard for traditional good taste. Meanwhile, the late fashion designer Patrick Kelly, had a passion for black dolls, statuettes and African figurines, and his Paris flat is another example of an unconventional collection gone wild; it practically became a shrine to black culture, with objects displayed on every possible surface as well as in special display cabinets. To provide the ultimate backdrop to his African-inspired collection, the floors were dotted with leopardskin rugs and the walls covered in yellow straw matting – the perfect example of a true passion for collecting taking over a home.

LEFT: KITSCH CAN WORK OUT OF CONTEXT – IN THIS CASE, A COLLECTION OF MICKEY MOUSE LUNCHBOXES IS JUXTAPOSED WITH THE CLEAN, MINIMAL LINES OF VERNER PANTON'S TULIP TABLE AND CHAIRS.

ABOVE LEFT AND ABOVE: SOMETIMES, IT'S A CASE OF THE BRASHER THE BETTER – FEEL FREE TO DISPLAY THE OBJECTS THAT YOU REALLY LIKE.

fashioning an inventive display

LEFT: STYLISH SHOP DISPLAYS CAN
BE A RICH SOURCE OF INSPIRATION
FOR THE ARTISTIC HOMEMAKER.

BELOW LEFT: FASHION DESIGNER AND
STYLIST ISABELLA BLOW DISPLAYS HER
HATS LIKE BEAUTIFUL SCULPTURES.

BELOW RIGHT: A HAT BY MILLINER
PHILIP TREACY BECOMES A BEAUTIFUL
FOCAL POINT IN ISABELLA BLOW'S
DRESSING ROOM.

Many of us have accumulated colourful collections of shoes and fashion accessories, so why not use them to create the ultimate in fashionable home art and display treasured pieces in an aesthetic way? You could, for instance, drape fabrics or display pieces of vintage clothing on dressmaker's dummies. In the bedroom or dressing room you could elevate shoes to art-gallery status by arranging them on open shelving systems, which would emphasize each pair. And as contemporary artists paint rows of handbags on their canvases, why not display real handbags in an equally aesthetically pleasing manner – either by hanging them in serried ranks directly on to the walls or arranging them in a neat row on a mantelpiece.

Not surprisingly, handbag designer Lulu Guinness uses bags as pieces of art in the interior of her west London home. Similarly, actress Ali McGraw displays her bags and shawls on her sitting-room walls when she's not using them, and model Helena Christiansen hangs her

favourite necklaces from nails on the walls of her
home and shows off her collection of shoes on
a stairway that leads to nowhere. A friend of
mine, who had a pile of expensive silk scarves
that she no longer wore, had them individually
framed to make a bold and beautifully
decorative feature on a white wall.

Stylish shop displays can be a rich source
of inspiration for the artistic homemaker.
A trip to shoemaker Manolo Blahnik's jewel
box of a shop in London, for example, reveals
all manner of inventive ways of displaying
shoes: a delicate red-beaded mule is nailed
to a wall; a glass display cabinet features
precious evening slippers; and shoes are
artfully arranged on padded silk footstools
and pedestals. There are even shoes hanging
from a picture rail.

Not only is Blahnik's shop a shoe fetishist's
delight, it is also a great example of a teasing
and humorous display, which illustrates how to
exhibit beautiful objects in unexpected places.

THE ART OF ASSEMBLAGE

You probably would not want to have Damien Hirst's cabinet full of steel surgical equipment in your sitting room. Nevertheless, it is proof that art gives us *carte blanche* to collect and display anything and everything – from the bizarre to the mundane. The key is to collect with conviction.

Remember, too, that, in some instances, quantity really is quality. You can take this idea of repetition and apply it to anything you care to collect, from teapots to handbags to garden tools. It was one of the principles adopted by the Pop artists of the 1950s and 1960s. Jim Dine's *Five Feet of Colourful Tools* (1962–3), which consisted of colourful household tools hung against an unprimed canvas, is the perfect example. Claes Oldenburg's *Pastry Case* (1961), which features nine plastic sculptures of ice-cream sundaes, chocolate gateaux and banana splits in a glass case, works on the same principle – that the whole is greater than the sum of its parts. Such work was validated by an influential exhibition, which took place in autumn 1961, entitled *The Art of Assemblage* and organized by the Museum of Modern Art in New York. This show effectively paved the way for other contemporary interpretations, including Hirst's cabinet of clinical curiosities.

You do not always need a multitude of items to make a statement, however. For example, Jeff Koons turned a solitary vacuum cleaner into a piece of art, called *New Hoover Convertible* (1980), simply by putting it in a display cabinet. Some recognized works of art even juxtapose unrelated objects: Pop artist Georges Brecht's *Repository* assemblage is a white wall cabinet containing such disparate objects as an abacus, a tennis ball, keys, toothbrushes and a Christmas-tree bauble. Though it sounds mad, this idea translates well into the domestic environment because you can justify making an assemblage of objects that mean something to you. You could even follow the lead of artist Joe Tilson, who asked his family and friends to donate *objets trouvés* to his *A–Z: A Contribution Picture* (1963), a construction in a wooden box. Alternatively, if you collect everyday objects, such as theatre or concert tickets, you can take inspiration from Joseph Cornell's shadow boxes, which displayed intimate, everyday vignettes, or the 'found-object' collages of Kurt Schwitters. Liberate your imagination, and you will be surprised by the highly personal collections you can create.

LEFT AND ABOVE: THE PRINCIPLE OF REPETITION – WHETHER IT BE GLASS TUMBLERS OR CHINA CATS – ILLUSTRATES THAT QUANTITY CAN MEAN QUALITY. IN ADDITION, THE UNEXPECTED SETTING ALSO ADDS TO THE IMPACT.

RIGHT: A SERIES OF MOULDED WAX HANDBAGS DISPLAYED ON LITTLE GLASS SHELVES CREATES AN INSTALLATION-LIKE EFFECT.

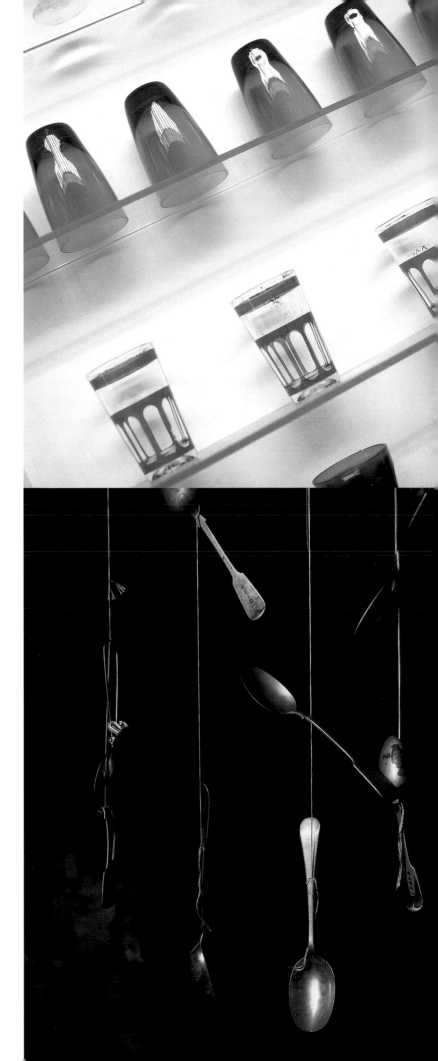

everyday objects as art: creating your own still-life

Beauty can be found in the most unlikely of objects. Artist and textile designer Carolyn Quartermaine displays empty champagne bottles in clear glass (Louis Roederer crystal, admittedly), for example, in front of a tarnished silver mirror. She has also amassed a collection of clear-glass decanters and vases on a mantelpiece to create a translucent still-life in her home. The trick is to arrange objects in groups as if they are about to be drawn. Often the simplest ideas have the biggest impact – a row of coloured silk coat hangers, for example, hanging on pegs on a bedroom wall, skeins of embroidery silks spilling out of a sewing box, or a collection of pottery displayed on open shelves.

Similarly, you can collect and display anything natural – foliage, sticks, stones – in an artistic way. Plunder the natural world to create your own impromptu still-lifes, and remember that you can change them according to the seasons with no expense involved: choose shells and pieces of driftwood in summer; berries and pine cones in the autumn. Look at how nature works with colour palettes and exploit the wealth of organic textures in your displays. Pebbles collected from the beach, for example, can be artfully displayed in spirals on the coffee table, creating domestic echoes of an Andy Goldsworthy piece.

sit on it; eat off it

'art is sexy!
art is money-sexy.
art is money-sexy-social climbing
fantastic!'

THOMAS HOVING, FORMER DIRECTOR OF THE
METROPOLITAN MUSEUM OF ART IN NEW YORK

THE FINE ART OF FURNITURE

Can something you sit on, eat off or work on be considered as art? Some people regard furniture as having less artistic merit than a painting or sculpture, and it may seem hard to get as excited over a side table as you might over a Seurat. Throughout history, however, furniture has served a decorative and artistic function: from the ornate pieces of Art Nouveau to the spare creations of the 1960s and 1970s. The fact that a plywood sculpture by Charles Eames recently sold at auction for £245,000 proves that furniture has achieved the heady status of fine art. The links between furniture, art and sculpture have been further reinforced by those artists, such as the sculptor Diego Giacometti, who straddle both worlds. American sculptor Danny Lane, whose stunning glass tables consist of slabs of glass arranged like a collage, is another good example. Unsurprisingly, the names of top furniture designers now carry as much cachet as those of famous artists.

Art is often said to cheer people up, and an elegant piece of furniture can lift the spirits and have just as much impact as an exquisite painting. Often, it is the style of the furniture, rather than the works of art on the wall, that you notice first on entering a home. Think also of how one piece of furniture – whether it is a wire chair or an inflatable plastic seat – can set the tone for an entire room. Furniture personalizes an environment and stamps your personality on it. It is for this reason that increasing numbers of people are prepared to invest in a sofa or chair by a contemporary name such as Marc Newson, whose elegant, sculptural creations are considered to be the essence of loft-style living. Many retailers are also taking a more arty approach. Habitat, for example, has employed Tom Dixon as head designer and has launched a range of furniture called Twentieth-Century Legends, reproducing designs dating from the 1960s and 1970s, by such luminaries as Verner Panton and Pierre Paulin.

Mirroring the current popularity of paintings from the 1960s and 1970s, there has recently been a huge explosion in demand for original pieces of furniture from that period. It also reflects the modern taste in interior design: funky, moulded plastic and futuristic metal is more popular today than old-fashioned mahogany and ormolu. Although Thomas Chippendale is the most famous name in English furniture design, image-conscious home-owners prize iconic designers such as Arne Jacobson, Charles Eames and Verner Panton more highly. Jacobson's Egg chair and Panton's moulded plastic stacking chairs have clean, sculptural qualities much more in keeping with the modern interior than a little Louis XIV something.

Few true modernists would relish the prospect of living with a set of eighteenth-century French salon furniture in their sitting room; such pieces belong to a life behind ropes in London's Victoria and Albert Museum, not in the progressive interior. Furniture by twentieth-century architects and artists such as Mies van der Rohe, Le Corbusier and Charles Eames, on the other hand, sits easily in the modern domestic setting. Le Corbusier's landmark piece, the Grand Confort chair – an elegant and compact cube shape designed in 1928 – looks as modern today as it did many decades ago. And who would not want to live with the organic lines of an amoeba-shaped Eames chair? We are likely to appreciate an Eames for its sculptural and aesthetic qualities as much as its functional attributes. And frankly, who cares if a chair is comfortable when it looks this good?

'Sofas are about sex, chilling out,
TV dinners, talking, sleeping.'

Matthew Hilton, furniture designer.

changing attitudes to furniture

During the Italian Renaissance little attention was paid to the design
and positioning of furniture because it was felt that it might detract
from the work of a great painter – surprising, perhaps, given the
Italian flair for furniture. In seventeenth-century France, on the other
hand, furniture was actively displayed and used as dazzling evidence of
wealth and splendour. Artist Charles Le Brun's decoration of the palace at
Versailles is the best example: he considered the accumulation of *objets
d'art*, furniture, paintings, panelling and wall hangings as a single entity,
designed to reflect the King's majesty. Furniture placed around the walls
was arranged in a formal, symmetrical manner, and the centre of the
room was usually kept clear. Comfort was a secondary consideration.
Today we view furniture somewhere between these extremes: the aim
is to balance beauty with functionality, as a room full of elegant but
uncomfortable furniture is pointless. As furniture designer Matthew
Hilton points out, you cannot afford to be too precious. 'Sofas are
about sex, chilling out, TV dinners, talking, sleeping,' he says.

ABOVE RIGHT: A MODERN APPROACH
TO FURNITURE LAYOUT.

RIGHT: WHEN INTRODUCING FURNITURE
INTO THE CONTEMPORARY HOME, THE
AIM IS TO TRY AND BALANCE BEAUTY
WITH FUNCTIONALITY.

FAR RIGHT: MATTHEW HILTON'S
'BALZAC' CHAIR AND FOOTSTOOL
COULD WELL BECOME COLLECTOR'S
ITEMS IN THE FUTURE.

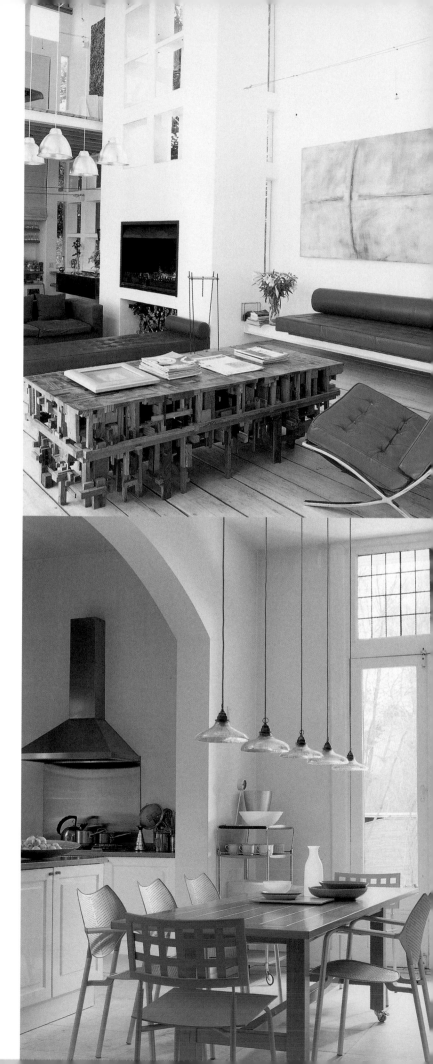

the art of living with furniture

Furniture is not as versatile or easy to live with as a picture: you cannot stow a table, chair or sofa in a cupboard when you tire of it. It can be hard, too, to live in a relaxed fashion with an expensive item of furniture, for the more pristine the condition the more valuable it is. Errant coffee cups and clumsy guests are a constant worry. It is for this reason that some people are wary of collecting furniture. The solution is to use one or two well-chosen pieces as an accent in a room rather than filling an entire living space with museum-quality pieces. You cannot lock a prized piece of furniture away in a glass case but you can place it strategically, somewhere where it is less likely to get harmed. You might, for instance, want to make a feature of a Marc Newson wooden chair in your living room. With any luck, if you position it away from the main seating area – tucked into a corner or a window bay, for instance – guests will take the hint that they can look but not lounge. Isolating a piece of furniture in this way also minimizes the chances of a drink being spilled over it.

LEFT: IF FURNITURE IS PRECIOUS, PLACE
IT STRATEGICALLY IN AN AREA OF THE
ROOM WHERE IT IS LESS LIKELY TO BE
HARMED — IN THIS CASE BEHIND SLIDING
GLASS DOORS.

by arrangement

Practical considerations aside, the way you arrange furniture in a room – even the colours that you choose – is a form of artistic expression. Consider, for example, the recent trend for Arne Jacobsen's Butterfly stacking chair (1945). Widely available, in a variety of colours, the impact of this piece varies from one interior to another depending on the colours the owner has chosen and how they work in the room. In this way, the chair becomes a brush of colour on a wider canvas. An empty room is effectively a giant three-dimensional canvas. Even the arrangement of beanbags around a rug can be considered as an artistic composition of sorts.

Shapes are also important. Curvy furniture is very fashionable at the moment (just think of Marc Newson's Embryo chair or Tom Dixon's famous S-chair), and works well in small rooms. Clever arranging also draws attention to an interesting piece of furniture. One of the best ways to do this is to display an item, such as a dining table, on a raised floor so that it becomes the focal point of a room. Stunning effects can be achieved by making a Perspex platform with fibre optic lighting underneath.

ABOVE RIGHT: A VERY MODERN COMPOSITION – THE CURVY LINES OF ARNE JACOBSEN'S 'SWAN' CHAIR AND PIERRE PAULIN'S 'TONGUE' CHAIR WORK WELL TOGETHER IN THIS SMALL SPACE.

RIGHT: ISOLATE A PIECE OF FURNITURE TO DRAW ATTENTION TO IT. THIS CHAIR IS FURTHER HIGHLIGHTED BY THE BLUE STRIP OF ILLUMINATED PERSPEX THAT HAS BEEN SET INTO THE FLOOR.

CONTEMPORARY COLLECTING:
SPOTTING THE CHARLES EAMES OF THE FUTURE

The most obvious choice for the discerning modern homeowner is the work of living designers. This is particularly exciting because it carries with it the potential for spotting a Mies van der Rohe of the future. Pieces by Marc Newson and Tom Dixon are already fetching large sums, while the Miss Blanche chair by Japanese architect Shiro Kurama – a staggeringly beautiful Perspex design embedded with delicate red roses – recently fetched £58,000 at auction. So how can you spot the pieces that will end up in museums and spark bidding wars in 50 years' time? It is worth bearing in mind that chairs, in particular, become iconic pieces of art. Two of the most important factors likely to affect any furniture's saleability in the future, meanwhile, are the designer's name and the rarity of the piece. The trick here is to search out the new and interesting, and focus on the names that generate media hype. Look out for limited-edition works, unusual designs and anything which defines a moment.

LEFT: VERNER PANTON'S WHITE MOULDED PLASTIC STACKING CHAIR HAS BECOME A MODERN CLASSIC. ITS CLEAN, CURVY LINES ARE PERFECT FOR THE CONTEMPORARY INTERIOR.

RIGHT: THE FLOWING ORGANIC SHAPE OF THIS CHAIR BY CHARLES EAMES WORKS WELL WITH A CURVED GLASS COFFEE TABLE FROM THE SAME ERA.

period collecting

Some serious accumulators of fine art view their furniture as an extension of their collecting and surround themselves with pieces of the same period and style. Certainly, there is a lot to be said for teaming like with like: ornately carved and elegant rococo furniture seems to be the natural accompaniment to blowzy rococo paintings; the hard-edged shape of a Le Corbusier armchair complements a Cubist painting from the same period; and a Marc Newson chair looks undeniably at home with a modern canvas.

Currently, furniture designed in the 1960s and 1970s is particularly fashionable among collectors. Moreover, working-class 1950s furniture, once regarded as ugly, is now highly prized in certain quarters. You should not be afraid, however, to mix designs from different stylistic periods. It is more important, when arranging furniture, to look at whether shapes and colours compete or complement each other than to create a rigidly coherent period collection.

RIGHT: TWO PRINTED-LINEN DESIGNS BY CAROLYN QUARTERMAINE, 'BLOSSOM' AND 'GINZA' (PART OF HER 'ORIENTAL SHADOWS' COLLECTION FOR SAHCO HESSLEIN) ARE USED TO COVER HER NINETEENTH-CENTURY CHAIR. THE FRAME FROM THE SAME PERIOD CONTAINS A PRINT, *ROSES*, BY TINA MODOTTI.

BELOW: MAKE A STRONG STATEMENT WITH PIECES OF THE SAME STYLE AND PERIOD – IN THIS CASE ANGULAR CHAIRS BY LE CORBUSIER.

MODERN ELECTICISM: USING OLD FURNITURE IN A MODERN SPACE

Close your eyes and imagine the visual impact of an antique French salon chair next to a Conran sofa in a light, wooden-floored apartment; or an ornate French mirrored dressing table in a simple, uncluttered bedroom. This 'magpie' approach – introducing a few quirky antiques into a minimalist living space – has become a major trend in interior design. Known as 'modern eclectic', it takes style, flair and imagination to mix furniture in this way but the result is artistic, individual, and often stunning. It is almost as though you are creating a three-dimensional collage. Artist and stylist Carolyn Quartermaine is known for the way she mixes furniture from different periods in a creative way – teaming a Louis XIV-style chair with a 1950s plastic Tulip table by Eero Saarinen, for example.

When you are incorporating old pieces of furniture into a modern space the challenge is to create equilibrium and balance between contemporary items and pieces from the past. The golden rule of modern eclecticism is not to force an excessive amount of furniture into the room. (Incidentally, the modern belief that less is more dates back to ancient Rome when sparsely furnished homes contained a few simple but ornate pieces of furniture.) The decorative schemes should be simple and uncluttered, too, and the background colour subtle, in order to allow the carefully chosen pieces to stand out. Think of it as being like making a soup: you do not want to throw too many rich ingredients or clashing flavours into the pan, or the end result will be unpalatable.

LEFT: A FEW WELL-CHOSEN PIECES – IN THIS CASE ANTIQUE FRENCH MIRRORS AND CHANDELIERS – LOOK STUNNING IN A MODERN SPACE. THE KEY TO MODERN ECLECTICISM IS TO KEEP THE DECORATIVE SCHEME SIMPLE AND UNCLUTTERED.

ABOVE: BEAUTIFULLY DECORATIVE ANTIQUE PIECES ADD CHARACTER TO AN OTHERWISE SPARE AND MINIMAL SPACE IN CAROLYN QUARTERMAINE'S HOME-CUM-SHOWROOM.

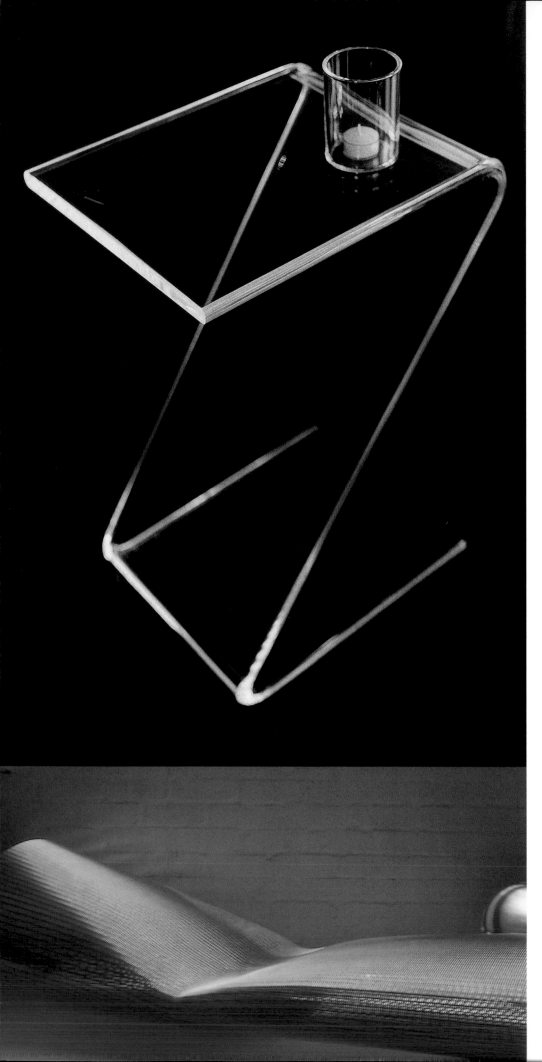

BUYING AND CARING FOR FURNITURE

buying contemporary

If you have deep pockets and an abiding passion for furniture, key pieces by well-known names currently exchange hands – often for tens of thousands of pounds – at top auction houses around the world. Nevertheless, the recent proliferation of shop-cum-galleries such as Viaduct, Vitra and SCP in London, all help to make buying cutting-edge designs easier. In addition, The Conran Shop, Heal's, and even some department stores, such as Selfridges, also stock a good selection of modern pieces, while Habitat, under the design direction of Tom Dixon, has made furniture inspired by designers such as Verner Panton and Pierre Paulin accessible to the masses.

As with painting and textile design, if you want to source new talent, college degree shows – particularly the Royal College of Art in London – are a good place to start. The most important event in the professional furniture designer's year, however, is the Milan Furniture Fair – a five-day trade exhibition which takes place every April. Here, new designs are unveiled for the first time (although serious collectors buy directly from the designer before the work is shown). Some trade exhibitions such as 100% Design in London, for example, are open to the general public for at least one day, and many exhibitors are happy to sell their work directly to the public.

TOP LEFT: CLEARLY MODERN – CURRENT
FURNISHING TASTE FAVOURS MINIMAL,
UNFUSSY DESIGN.

LEFT: GOOD CONTEMPORARY-STYLE
FURNITURE IS BECOMING INCREASINGLY
EASY TO FIND.

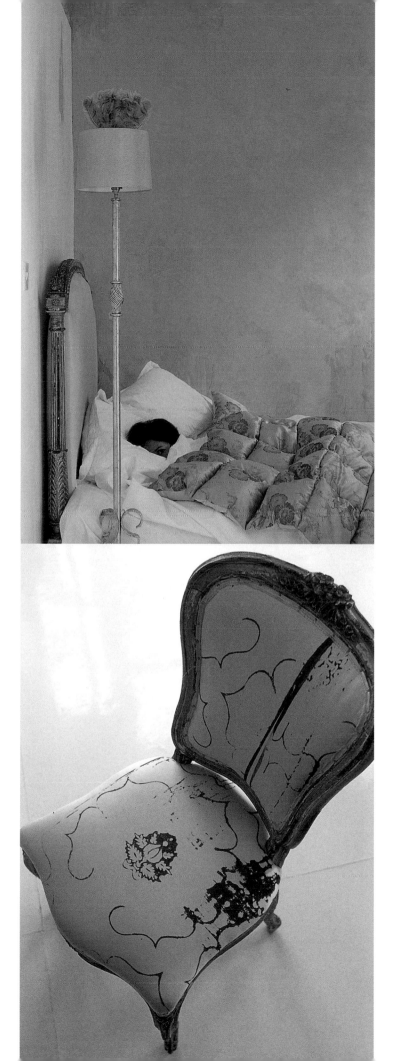

buying antique furniture

Furniture is a genre of artistic endeavour which is particularly prone to fakes, so do not take anything at face value. As with all forms of art, knowledge is the key to avoid being duped. Books can help you to identify and date pieces of interest, as will visits to major museums. The Victoria and Albert Museum in London and the Metropolitan Museum of Art in New York both house extensive collections of furniture.

Auctions are a good source of period furniture, but it is important to remember to do your research beforehand, and to decide on your price limit in order to prevent yourself from getting carried away by sale-room fever. In addition to the well-known auction houses, it may be worthwhile visiting smaller ones in the country, where it is perfectly possible to pick up a solid oak Art Deco dining table for as little as £200, if you look hard enough.

If you plan to spend a large amount of money on a period item and you want to make sure you are buying the real thing, it is best to go to a dealer – often an intimidating experience as they tend to be located in scarily exclusive shopping streets. They are, however, likely to be the best bet if you are seeking a pristine example of a certain item. Make sure that your dealer is reputable: most belong to a professional organization.

Foraging in flea markets is the way to have the most fun when you are seeking out antique furniture, particularly if chandeliers, gilt mirrors and chairs are on your shopping list. The downside to trawling flea markets is the fact that they are also favoured by professionals, who descend at dawn in their droves in order to pick up highly-prized mirrored French furniture (dressing tables are particularly popular), sleigh beds and tapestry armchairs, and pay half the price quoted by a dealer. As a result, it is becoming increasingly difficult for the amateur to find a bargain. There are 30 or so good antiques fairs in France but dealers keep the addresses a closely-guarded secret. The only answer is to become best friends with a dealer – but even so, they might not divulge such confidential information!

LEFT AND ABOVE LEFT :
CERTAIN PIECES OF ANTIQUE
FRENCH FURNITURE ARE PRIZED BY
MODERNISTS, AS EXEMPLIFIED IN
CAROLYN QUARTERMAINE'S
BEDROOM, ABOVE LEFT; A CHAIR,
LEFT, IS UPHOLSTERED IN SILK-
SATIN, HAND-PAINTED BY HER.

taking care of your furniture

Wooden furniture should be dusted often and also requires regular waxing with a good polish. This moisturizes and nourishes the wood as well as providing a pleasing sheen. It is worth noting that spray polishes often create a patchy finish and cause residues to build up, and should therefore be avoided. Changes in temperature can cause wood to expand, contract and split, so it is best to avoid placing wooden furniture near sources of heat or beside windows which are continually opened and closed. Veneered furniture is particularly susceptible to changes in climatic conditions.

Plastic, Perspex and laminated wood furniture, meanwhile, can be wiped down with a damp cloth. If you are in any doubt – or if the piece is made from metal or an unusual material – check with the supplier first.

FURNITURE AS PURE ART

The late Donald Judd intended his minimalist furniture to be both viewed in a gallery and then used at home. Other artistic furniture creations, such as Pop artist Allen Jones's erotic coffee table, which incorporates a female mannequin on all fours wearing fetishistic gear, could be used in the home, so long as your friends are broad-minded. Some pieces, however, such as Scott Burton's chaise longues in marble or granite, are clearly designed for public rather than domestic spaces.

Several contemporary artists are working with furniture almost as a medium. Tracey Emin's bed and Damien Hirst's medical cabinet are the best examples. Artist Jane Simpson, who specializes in rubber sculptures and domestic objects that appear to have been frosted with ice, trawls flea markets for furniture that can be transformed into art. Her *Ice Table* and *Ice Shelf* are the ultimate in cool, three-dimensional art. Such pieces can work well in a home but they should be treated as sculpture with enough surrounding space to be appreciated properly. Sometimes people will buy a furniture-as-art item purely for their own enjoyment – and these need not necessarily be displayed at all. Architect Sophie Hicks treasures a porcelain bathroom sink by Hadrian Pigott, bought by her husband in a Charles Saatchi sale at Christie's. Rather than being used or displayed prominently, the sink is contained in a case lined with purple velvet.

LEFT: THE ART OF WOOD – IT'S IMPORTANT TO ALWAYS TAKE CARE OF YOUR FURNITURE.

ABOVE RIGHT: IS IT A SOFA, A TOOLBOX OR AN INSTALLATION? THE ANSWER IS ACTUALLY ALL THREE.

BELOW: ART FOR ART'S SAKE – ALLEN JONES'S 'FETISH' CHAIR FROM THE 1960S.

RIGHT: THIS INTERIOR IS PURE POP ART – FROM THE FURNITURE TO THE PRINTS.

the gods of mod:
icons of twentieth-century furniture design

Certain furniture designers are as famous as top artists, and many of their pieces still look up-to date, despite being decades old.

- **Alvar Aalto** (1898–1976) The first furniture designer to use plywood. Key piece: curved armchair (1930) made of a single piece of moulded plywood.

- **Charles Eames** (1907–78) Often in collaboration with his wife Ray, Eames used new moulding techniques to produce some of the most innovative furniture of the twentieth century. Key piece: one-piece fibreglass Shell chair (1948) in a flowing organic shape (left).

- **Eileen Gray** (1878–1976) Architect and designer, Gray became a pioneer of modern design in the 1920s, turning her hand to geometric rugs and furniture. Using screens as room-dividers, she pioneered one of loft-living's tenets. Key piece: multi-functional lacquered cabinet (1923).

- **Arne Jacobsen** (1902–71) One of Denmark's first modernists, the work of this architect has stood the test of time. Key pieces: Butterfly stacking chair (1945), available in a wide variety of colours, and one of the most popular pieces of furniture in the modern home. Also the Egg chair (1958), a moulded fibreglass shell on a swivelling metal base. His Swan chair (1957–8, right) has stood the test of time.

- **Kaara Klint** (1888–1954) trained as a painter but worked as an architect and furniture designer. His fondness for plain textiles and unvarnished wood led to him being regarded as the father of modern Danish design. Key piece: the Safari (1933) chair.

- **Florence Knoll** (b. 1917) After studying architecture she joined Hans Knoll to set up an interior design service in 1943. Although she manufactured some classic designs such as Mies van der Rohe's Barcelona chair (1929) and Eero Saarinen's Womb chair (1947–8), she also did a great deal of designing for the office market.

- **Le Corbusier** (1887–1965) A name synonymous with minimalist architecture and elegant furniture, in which pure form reflected pure function (above left). Key piece: the Grand Confort (1928), a compact armchair in the shape of a cube with a chromium-plated frame. Also known for his chaise longue (1928), which was ergonomically designed to fit the human body, and is still a popular piece today.

- **Verner Panton** (b. 1926) Danish designer who created the world's first one-piece, cantilevered chair, (1960), made from a fibreglass shell. Key piece: Panton stacking chair (1965), a moulded plastic chair (left).

- **Mies van der Rohe** (1886–1969) Practised as an architect, but also known for the elegantly functional furniture he developed at the Bauhaus. Key piece: the Barcelona chair (1929), comprising a steel frame with leather upholstery and accompanying footstool.

ornaments and accessories

'life is enhanced by art'

RENE SASSELIN

ACCESSORIES AS OBJECTS OF ART

Just about every aspect of home furnishings has become subject to artistic scrutiny. For example, lighting, once a purely functionable notion, has become increasingly concerned with artistic statement, with the traditional standard lamp being outshone by decorative columns, curtains of light and globes resembling radiant sculptures. Plates, too, come in interesting and unusual shapes nowadays; or feature beautiful naive leaf or flower motifs, transforming the dining table into an artistic statement. Philippe Starck, meanwhile, has transformed the most mundane of implements, including scales and corkscrews, into art forms. His famous Alessi lemon squeezer – the 'must-have' kitchen accessory of the 1980s – is prized more for its sculptural good looks than its ability to extract juice from lemons. While some objects are intrinsically beautiful, others are elevated to the status of art over time Even industrial designs – toasters, radios and blenders from the 1920s, for example, have now been recognized as works of artistic prominence and therefore become collectable.

ABOVE: EVEN THE MOST MUNDANE HOUSEHOLD OBJECTS CAN BE ELEVATED TO THE STATUS OF ART WITH THE PASSAGE OF TIME.

LEFT: GLASS TUMBLERS CAN HAVE AN INTRINSIC BEAUTY.

ABOVE RIGHT: MAKE A VISUAL STATEMENT WITH YOUR FAVOURITE BOOKS BY DISPLAYING THEM ARTFULLY.

RIGHT: BOOKS WITH PRETTY, DECORATIVE COVERS CAN BE USED AS DISPLAY OBJECTS.

collecting and displaying books

Books – whether precious first editions or stylish tomes of black-and-white photography -— have become a popular form of domestic art. More people collect books than anything else, and it is surprising how many stylish rooms are packed with them. Books do not exist just to be read. They are also a great way of embellishing a living space and expressing individual taste, which is what art in the home is all about. Indeed, some people buy books simply as objects of artistic merit. New York boutique owner Laurie McLendon, for example, admits to buying books in languages she can't read – choosing them purely for their beautiful covers. Equally, you could build up a collection of books on your favourite artist. American art collector Herbert Schimmel established a library of over 6,000 books relating to Toulouse-Lautrec and the period in which he worked.

Certain books really catch the eye: the brightly patterned blue, green and purple cover of a book on fashion designer Emilio Pucci is now a collector's item. *Casa Mexicana* by Tim Street-Porter is another example. Its arresting pink cover has strong overtones of the artist Frida Kahlo and is far too beautiful to be hidden away on a book shelf.

The way that the books are displayed can also become an art form. A wall, or even just a couple of shelves of colourful books behind a bed can create an attractive focal point, while art books displayed on a coffee table act as a form of horizontal decoration. (If you are feeling inventive, you could lay a sheet of glass over the top of a pile of books to create a makeshift coffee table and also protect the books.) Generally, however, people display their books on shelves. It is worth remembering that in this case the quality of the shelving is all-important. Innovative designs that curl in a loop around the wall, for example, will turn a book display into a funky design feature. Nowadays, chunky, low-level book shelving is particularly popular. You can buy this relatively inexpensive shelving from Ikea and paint it in any colour you choose. At the other end of the scale, there are companies specializing in made-to-measure and custom-built bookcases. You can also get special angled shelving, which allows you to display a particularly beautiful book flat to give it more prominence. Alternatively, you could prop up a selection of art books on top of a chest – or even on the floor. Although some homes have books stacked up on every available surface it is preferable, in modern interiors, to create a feeling of space, punctuating shelves with small pictures, sculptures or interesting *objets d'art*. Other useful tips include removing gaudy dust jackets in order to create a richer palette of book spines, or replacing dust covers with uniform white covers. The most important point to remember is that hip hardbacks look attractive, while ratty, tatty paperbacks do not.

SEXY CERAMICS

In the past, pottery and ceramics have been considered one of the more esoteric – and least sexy – areas of the art world. It is easy to feel passionate about a painting, but much harder to get fired up about a bowl or a pot. Attitudes are changing, however. Quite simply, today's pots are hot – not any old commercially-produced pot, bowl or vase, mind, but one-off, hand-thrown pieces. Whether you opt for a dark, rough-textured bowl that appears to have come directly from an archaeological dig, or a vase that is pale, porcelain perfection, using ceramics to make an artistic statement in the home is becoming more and more popular. They are also more affordable than paintings. A small dish by an established name can cost as little as £25, while £5,000 will buy you a good piece by a famous potter.

The real area of interest for the modern homeowner is the work of a new wave of funky, modern potters. Their ceramics are curvy, cool and organic in shape – unblemished by floral patterns or cutesy animal motifs. King of the cool ceramic is internationally acclaimed potter Jonathan Adler, whose work manages to be eye-catching, while at the same time retaining an integral and understated serenity. His shop in New York's fashionable SoHo does a brisk trade with hip Manhattan loft dwellers. Edmund de Waal's lopsided beakers, Sarah Jane Selwood's smooth shapes and Anna Silverton's overscaled curvaceous bowls are also typical of this new genre of collectable pottery. It is all a far cry from the patterned Limoges dinner services and ostentatious eighteenth-century Sèvres porcelain.

LEFT AND RIGHT: ANNA SILVERTON'S
CURVACEOUS CREAM POTS ARE
TYPICAL OF THE NEW BREED OF
MODERN, COLLECTABLE CERAMICS.

Picassos of the pot world

At the same time, there has been a revival of interest in the work of famous potters from the past. The most notable is Clarice Cliff, whose hand-painted, colourful designs from the 1920s and 1930s now enjoy cult status and are hotly pursued by collectors. Cliff painted freehand on pottery, creating everything from Cubist-inspired patterns to abstract designs, using a palette of citrus orange, cornflower blue, acid yellow, purple, red and green, often against a stark, white background. She also engaged several well-known artists to paint their designs onto pottery – a project which led to an exhibition called Modern Art For The Table, staged at Harrods in 1934. Although many of Clarice Cliff's colourful designs were considered too extreme at that time, the 1960s brought a reappraisal of her work. Throughout the 1970s and 1980s, with the resurgence of interest in Art Deco, both interest and prices spiralled upwards and Cliff's designs are now collected with passion.

The late Bernard Leach – Britain's foremost early studio potter – also had a talent for painting designs freehand on pottery. Leach was massively influential during the first half of the twentieth century, not only for his use of oriental decorative techniques such as raku (a crackle glaze), but also because he helped elevate the status of potters from mere artisan-craftsmen to artists. Simple and subtle in shape, Leach's pots were characterized by similarly low-key glazes and motifs. They are now considered collector's pieces, as are the works of many of his students, including his wife Janet, his son David, and Keith Murray. St Ives in Cornwall, where Leach established his work, is still one of the foremost places for ceramics.

displaying ceramics in the modern home

There are endless ways to make a modern statement with ceramics: a windowsill adorned with black bowls as smooth as pebbles; a collection of cream-coloured pots on a glass shelf; or one solitary vase spotlighted in a wall recess. Alternatively, you could try grouping together loose combinations of shapes – organic with geometric, for example – on a sideboard or a shelf devoted specifically to the display. Remember that the impact of a stunning artefact is lost if it is squeezed between books or CDs on an overcrowded surface. To form a homogeneous impression, you should select ceramics that share similarities in shape, colour or materials – and each one should be deliberately chosen.

WHAT TO LOOK FOR WHEN BUYING CONTEMPORARY POTTERY AND CERAMICS

- Pale glazes (white or cream) will always look cool and refined, and are more versatile than bright colours.
- Simple, sculptural shapes have by far the most artistic merit in the modern home.
- Don't be put off if a piece of pottery looks a bit haphazard or is not entirely symmetrical; such irregularities are often part of the appeal.
- Tall, skinny cylindrical vases are very much in vogue. For maximum effect, group several of them   ideally of different heights – together.
- Pots, vases and bowls with minimal decoration can have the most impact. Look for abstract daubs and simple, subtle motifs reflecting a Zen-Japanese influence.
- Raku and crackle glazes – where the piece looks as if it is cracked in many places – are very popular.
- According to pottery expert Veronica Manussis of Cobra & Bellamy, 'You should buy what you like, trust your eye and go for the best that you can afford.'

FAR LEFT: FLOWING ORGANIC SHAPES ARE IDEAL FOR DISPLAY IN THE CONTEMPORARY INTERIOR.

TOP LEFT: GROUP TALL, SKINNY VASES TOGETHER FOR A BOLD DISPLAY. THESE DESIGNS ARE BY RUPERT SPIRA.

LEFT: CYLINDRICAL POTS OF VARYING HEIGHTS, AGAIN BY RUPERT SPIRA, WORK WELL WHEN THEY ARE CLUSTERED TOGETHER LIKE THIS.

THE ART OF LIGHT

The traditional silhouette of the standard lamp is rapidly becoming obsolete; increasingly, lighting is taking on a sculptural quality in the home. Certain modern lights, such as Margaret O'Rorke's light sculptures, are almost like installations and create an instant focal point for a room. Similarly, Michael Sodeau's contemporary basket light fittings, made from hand-woven Indonesian cane, are designed to be displayed in clusters like an installation; while Tom Dixon's hugely successful Jack Light is a lamp, a table (with a piece of glass on top) and a work of art, all at the same time. It not only adds a warm shot of colour and light to a room but becomes a major feature.

Lighting is a very powerful medium that can be used to brilliant decorative effect. It also offers more scope for individual creativity. Tse Tse's fashionable paper cube lights, for example, look stunning when hung vertically on a wall – above the bed, say – to create a curtain of light and colour. The stick light is another recent and stylish innovation; mimimal and modern, it comes in a fantastic array of colours including orange, candy-pink, red and turquoise. They are relatively inexpensive so you can group several together in a variety of artistic ways. You can also create a wall of light and give a room a futuristic glow using Perspex sheets illuminated by fluorescent strip lights. All you have to do is prop up large sheets of translucent Perspex and place lights on the floor behind the screen; red Perspex gives a room a particularly rosy glow. Used with confidence and aplomb, even fairy lights can be employed to artistic effect – witness the famous British *Vogue* picture of model Kate Moss in a grungy bedroom with a string of fairy lights fixed with masking tape to the wall behind her.

You can achieve truly stunning effects with fibre-optic lighting. This is ideal for purely decorative lighting and can be used to create panels of light in the floor or walls, when laid under Perspex or glass – although you will need help from an experienced electrician. Because there are no bulbs to blow, it can be fitted in quite inaccessible places. Innovative lighting not only transforms a room but can also be used as a temporary work of art, to be turned on or off at the flick of a switch.

TOP: A 'NET' OF LITTLE LIGHTS CAN HAVE A STRONG IMPACT IN AN UNEXPECTED PLACE.

ABOVE: TOM DIXON'S 'JACK LIGHT' DOUBLES UP AS A LAMP AND ARTWORK.

RIGHT: CLEVER LIGHTING CAN BE AN ARTISTIC FEATURE IN ITSELF. IN THIS ULTRA-MODERN APARTMENT, COLOURED STRIPS HAVE BEEN SET INTO THE CEILING.

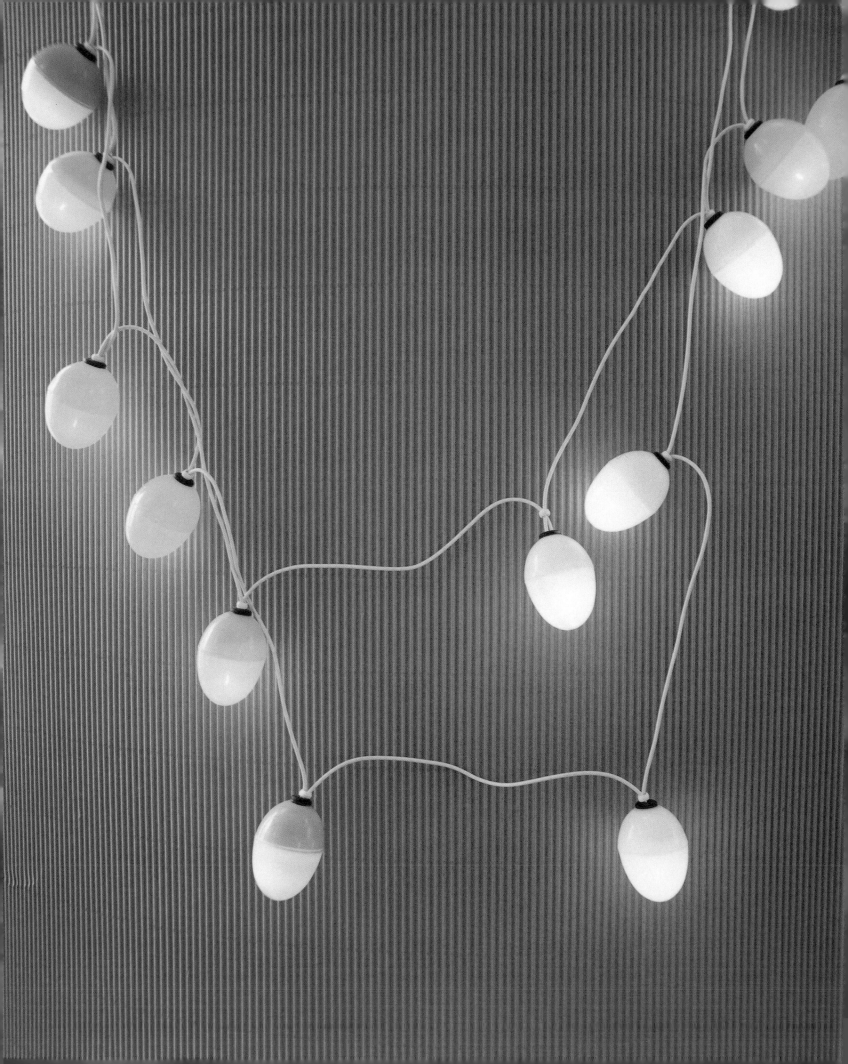

LEFT: A STRING OF EGG-SHAPED BULBS
IN DIFFERENT COLOURS CREATES AN
INNOVATIVE DISPLAY.

BELOW LEFT: CUBED PAPER LIGHTS
HAVE LOTS OF ARTISTIC POTENTIAL.

BELOW RIGHT: A CLEVER INSTALLATION
FEATURING A BOWL OF ILLUMINATED BULBS.

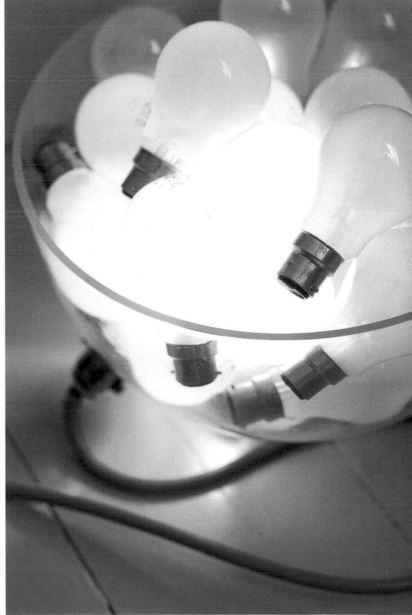

ART OF GLASS

Glass is one of the most beautiful artistic mediums although, until fairly recently, collecting glassware was regarded as a bit flashy (glance at the exotically coloured Art Nouveau creations by Louis Comfort Tiffany and you will see why). The minimal beauty of contemporary glass design, however, means that today glass is undergoing a renaissance and many people are becoming avid collectors. Modern or antique, glass has immense presence and offers an extraordinary range of colours and shapes. Whether you go to an auction and purchase an antique Murano wine goblet with decorative rosebuds twisting up the stem, buy one of Venini's famous Handkerchief fluted vases, or choose a sleek, modern bowl from The Conran shop, you will find that glass can look stunning in the contemporary home.

You can collect and display glass in many different ways. You could, for example, accumulate a variety of glass objects in a dazzling rainbow of colours and display them *en masse*, either on open shelves or in a special display cabinet. Alternatively, you might decide to limit yourself to one particular shade to complement or add colour to the decor of a room. Imagine, for example, the impact of a line-up of bright yellow vases and glassware on a white mantelpiece in an all-white room.

Some people collect by genre: glass candlesticks, vases or animals. Lalique's small colourful glass fish are particularly collectable and would make a dramatic bathroom display. You might, on the other hand, decide to invest in just one fantastic glass vase or sculpture to add a bold shot of colour to a room, or to act as centrepiece. A one-off piece by glass sculptor Anthony Stern, whose work is displayed in London's Victoria and Albert Museum, would be ideal for this purpose. Featuring swirling colours, Stern's Sky bowls are breathtakingly unique works of art, which he describes as 'abstract paintings in glass'. Interestingly, they have been bought by Japanese Buddhists as meditative objects for a Zen monastery.

You do not need to look to the past to find unique pieces of glass because many contemporary designs have the potential to become the collectables of the future. In addition to modern pieces by historical names such as Lalique and Venini – often made by the same masters who produced the collectables of 30 years ago – there are new glass artists coming to the fore and seeking them out can be fun. One such name is Amy Cushing, whose London-based company Mosquito Design produces exquisite glass tiles. Cushing also uses Murano glass to hand-produce vases and tableware, and undertakes commissions for glass installations in private interiors. Although it can cost thousands of pounds to buy a vase or sculpture by a top name, you can also find attractive pieces of art glass for less than £100.

LEFT: A MINI DISPLAY OF DELICATE AND DECORATIVE GLASS IS ARRANGED ON A CLEAR PERSPEX TABLE.

TOP: GLASS 'POP' VASE BY LA MURRINA.

ABOVE: CHOOSE GLASS OBJECTS IN A COLOUR THAT COMPLEMENTS YOUR ROOM, LIKE THESE NAXOS VASES BY LA MURRINA.

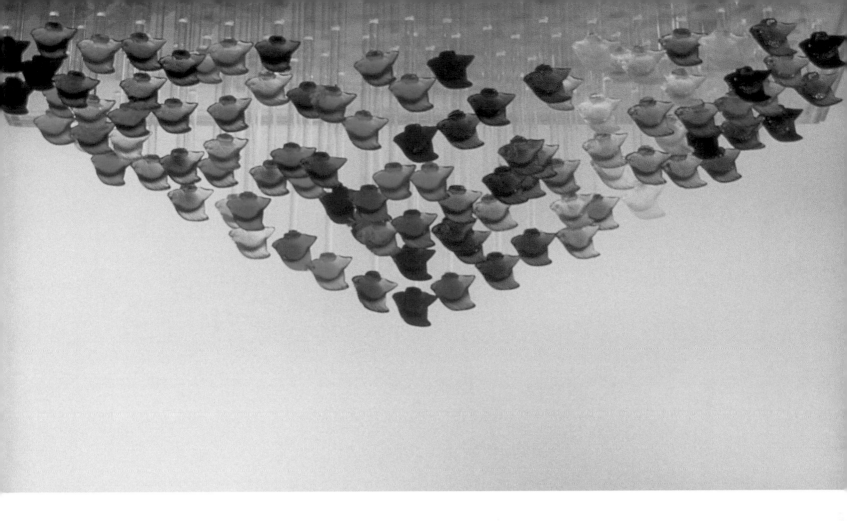

master glass artists: Lalique and Venini

Glass addicts may progress from one 'find' in a flea market to collecting prized pieces by Lalique and Venini, two of the names most synonymous with art glass. French-born René Lalique was an outstanding artist and craftsman, and is definitely considered the greatest of all the Art Nouveau glass-makers. He began working with glass in the 1890s and produced glass sculptures and statues, scent bottles, chandeliers, paperweights and jewellery, as well as vases and bowls. Lalique's descendants continued the tradition after his death and the company still creates interesting and stylish glass artefacts today.

Italian glass designer Paolo Venini is another name that is inextricably linked with twentieth-century art glass. He encouraged collaboration between artists and designers for over 70 years and during the 1940s Venini was the foremost name in decorative and coloured glass in Europe. Although he died in 1959, the Venini factory continues to flourish today.

Venini himself experimented with innovative, asymmetrical forms, the most famous being his Handkerchief vase, the fluted sides of which resemble a handkerchief blown upwards. Boldly striped, interestingly shaped or internally decorated, Venini pieces have become highly prized for their pattern, colours and delicate beauty.

ABOVE: A COLLECTION OF LALIQUE
GLASS FISHES IN DIFFERENT COLOURS
MAKES A STRIKING DISPLAY.

FAR LEFT: A COLLECTION OF ORNAMENTAL
GLASSES BY LA MURRINA.

TOP LEFT: SMALL 'MALIBU' VASE
BY LA MURRINA.

LEFT: DECORATIVE 'FOLLIE' VASES
BY LA MURRINA.

mirror image

A mirror with a decorative frame can transform a bare wall and act as a focal point in a room as well as creating an impression of more space. With a little artistic flair, you can achieve stunning effects with mirrors. Flea markets and auction rooms are a good source of ornate French gilded mirrors, and you can transform a minimalist interior by hanging a resplendent rococo mirror on a coloured wall (for some reason, gilt always looks particularly stunning against lilac or rich cornflower blue).

If rococo leaves you cold and gold leaf is not your style, you could try gathering up a selection of contemporary designs in different geometric shapes and stacking them on a wall vertically, one above the other. You could even turn a wall into a mirrored mosaic using bevelled mirrors of different shapes and sizes. Choose the mirror to suit the space: exploiting the curves of a round mirror, for example, can break up the straight lines of a boxy, rectangular room. Alternatively, you might like to commission a mirror for a particular room.

LEFT: A BEAUTIFUL ORNATE MIRROR SUCH AS THIS ONE IN ISABELLA AND DETMAR BLOW'S HOME CAN HAVE AS MUCH IMPACT ON A WALL AS A PAINTING.

RIGHT: CREATE A REFLECTIVE MOSAIC USING MIRRORS OF DIFFERENT SHAPES AND SIZES.

sculpture and installations

In the 1960s Verner Panton's psychedelic room installations were viewed in the same way as conceptual art is today. Sculptural, undulating forms created complete environments for the home; you had no control over aspects such as colour, shape and form. Installations are currently enjoying a renewed vogue, although large-scale pieces, like those produced by Damien Hirst, are more suited to commercial premises, such as office foyers and restaurants, than domestic spaces. That said, the established trend for loft-living means that a growing number of people can accommodate large sculptures or installations in their home. The key thing to remember is an uncluttered space lends weight to the objects on view.

RIGHT: PLACE STATUES AND SCULPTURES IN A HALLWAY SURROUNDED BY LOTS OF SPACE FOR MAXIMUM IMPACT.

BELOW: CREATED BY JIBBY BEANE, THIS LIGHT INSTALLATION DROPS FROM A SILVER SCULPTURE ALONG THE FLOOR OF HER APARTMENT.

DIRECTORY

antiques
professional associations
Antique Collectors Club
5 Church Street
Woodbridge
Suffolk IP12 1DS
Tel: 01394 385501
www.antique-acc.com

The British Antique Dealers Association
(20 Rutland Gate
London SW7 1BD
Tel: 020 7589 4128
www.bada.org

London and Provincial Antique Dealers
Association
Suite 214
535 King's Road
London SW10 0SZ
Tel: 020 7589 4128
www.bada.org

antique dealers
Alfie's Antique Market
13–25 Church Street
London NW8 8DT
Tel: 020 7723 6066
Everything from old dolls and toys to art
deco, glass, silver and ceramics.

Judy Greenwood Antiques
657 Fulham Road
London SW6 5PY
Tel: 020 7736 6037
Deals in French furniture, mirrors and
lighting, from 1870 to 1920.

art galleries
Here are a few galleries that are
particularly interesting. Ring to make
an appointment first.

Asprey Jacques
4 Clifford Street
London W1X 1RB
Tel: 020 7287 7675
www.aspreyjacques.com

Jibby Beane
www.jibbybean.com
Interesting modern pieces.

The Contemporary Art Gallery
123 Kennington Road
London SE11 6SF
Tel: 020 7735 8292
www.daniellearnaud.com
Owner Danielle Arnaud has some very
interesting artists, whose works she
displays in her living space and gallery.

Marlborough Fine Art
6 Albermarle Street
London W1X 4BY
Tel: 020 7629 5161
www.marlboroughfineartinc.com
Lithographs and limited edition prints
by well-known names like Victor Pasmore.

Modern Art Inc
74 Redchurch Street
London E2 7DJ
Tel: 020 7739 2081
www.modernartinc.com
Co-owned by Detmar Blow and Stuart
Shave, this gallery has an interesting
selection of contemporary artists.

The Saatchi Gallery
98 Boundary Road
London NW8 0RH
Tel: 020 7624 8299
Resolutely modern, this gallery features
the work of cutting-edge artists.

White Cube
44 Duke Street
London SW1Y 6DD
Tel: 020 7930 5373
www.whitecube.com
Represents cutting-edge artists like
Damien Hirst and Tracey Emin.

The Whitechapel Art Gallery
80–2 Whitechapel High Street
London E1 7QX
Tel: 020 7522 7888
www.whitechapel.org
A great place to view the work of
up-and-coming artists.

Wiseman Originals
34 West Square
London SE11 4SP
Tel: 020 7587 0747
www.wisemanoriginals@compuserve.com
Modern artists' work displayed in a
domestic setting. (By appointment only.)

art supplies
uk
Atlantis Art Materials
7–9 Plumber's Row
London E1 1EQ
Tel: 020 7377 8855
www.atlantis.co.uk
One of the largest art supply stores in
Europe; from brushes to easels.

Cowling & Wilcox
26 Broadwick Street
London W1V 1FG
Tel: 020 7734 9557
www.cowlingandwilcox.com
Good-quality brushes, papers and paints.

Falkiner Fine Papers
76 Southampton Row
London WC1B 4AR
Tel: 020 7831 1151
A beautiful selection of handmade papers
from around the world.

Lawrence
117–19 Clerkenwell Road
London EC1R 5BY
Tel: 020 7242 3534
www.lawrence.co.uk
Offers a huge range of canvases, papers,
brushes and paints.

Paperchase Products Ltd
213 Tottenham Court Road
London W1P 9AF
Tel: 020 7467 6200

usa
Kate's Paperie
561 Broadway
New York 10012
Tel: (1) 800-809 9880
Has a good selection of art papers,
including Japanese and handmade.

New York Central Art Supply
62 Third Avenue
New York 1003
Tel: (1) 212 473 7705
A wide variety of conventional art papers
and boards.

Pearl Paint Supply Company Inc
308 Canal Street
New York 10013
Tel: (1) 800 221 6845
Stocks papers, boards and fabric paints.

auction houses
uk
Bonhams
65–9 Lots Road,
London SW7 1HH
Tel: 020 7393 3900
www.bonhams.com

Christie's
8 King Street
London SW1Y 6QT
Tel: 020 7839 9060
www.christies.com
This particular branch offers thirteen
categories of fine art and furniture.

Christie's
85 Old Brompton Road
London SW7 3LD
Tel: 020 7581 7611
Sells paintings of less value as well
as collectables/memorabilia.

Sotheby's
34 New Bond Street
London W1A 2AA
Tel: 020 7293 5000
www.sothebys.com

usa
Christie's
502 Park Avenue
New York 10022
Tel: (1) 212 546 1000
www.christies.com

Christie's East
219 East 67th Street
New York 10021
Tel: (1) 212 606 0400

Christie's Los Angeles
360 North Camden Drive
Beverly Hills, California 90210
Tel: (1) 310 385 2600

Sotheby's
1334 York Avenue
New York 10021
Tel: (1) 212 606 7000
www.sothebys.com

buying photographs
Atlas Gallery
55–7 Tabernacle Street
London EC2A 4AA
Tel: 020 7490 4540

Hamiltons
13 Carlos Place
London W1Y 5AG
Tel: 020 7499 9493
www.hamiltonsgallery.com

The Photographers' Gallery
5 Great Newport Street
London WC2H 7HY
Tel: 020 7831 1772
www.photonet.org.uk

commissioning one-off pieces
The following organizations will be able
to help or point you in the right direction:

Contemporary Applied Arts
2 Percy Street
London W1P 9FA
Tel: 020 7436 2344
www.caa.org.uk
Offers a full commissioning service and
information on many makers.

The Crafts Council
44a Pentonville Road
London N1 9BY
Tel: 020 7278 7700
www.craftscouncil.org.uk

home accessories
La Murrina
79 Ebury Street
London SW1W 0NZ
Tel: 020 7730 7922
Striking glass designs.

Anna Silverton
Tel: 01588-650588 for stockists.
Modern handthrown vases and pots.

Michael Sodeau Partnership
25d Highgate West Hill
London N6 6NP
Tel: 020 7833 5020
Innovative lighting and other home
accessories. A name to watch.

Rupert Spira
Tel: 01588-650588 for stockists.
Fabulous ceramics.

Anthony Stern Glass
unit 205, Avro House
Havelock Terrace
London SW8 4AL
Tel: 020 7622 9463
Stern's stunning glassware is deemed
very collectable.

modern furniture sources

Aero
46 Weir Road
London SW19 8UG
Tel: 020 8971 0022 (enquiries);
020 8971 0066 (mail order)
www.aero-furniture.co.uk
Contemporary furniture for home and
office, also good home accessories.

The Conran Shop
81 Fulham Road
London SW3 6RD
Tel: 020 7589 7401
www.conran.co.uk
A good range of contemporary furniture,
much of it by well-known names.

Habitat
196 Tottenham Court Road
London W1P 9LD
Tel: 020 7255 2545
www.habitat.net
The Twentieth-Century Legends collection
includes designs by Verner Panton and
Pierre Paulin, among others.

Harrods Ltd
Knightsbridge
London SW1X 7XL
Tel: 020 7730 1234
www.harrods.com
Opened in early 2000; everything from
Tom Dixon to Arne Jacobsen.

Purves & Purves
80–1 and 83 Tottenham Court Road
London W1P 9HD
Tel: 020 7580 8223
www.purves.co.uk
Modern furniture and home accessories.

SCP
135 Curtain Road
London EC2A 3BX
Tel: 020 7739 1869
www.scp.co.uk
Contemporary furniture, including
reproductions of modern classics.

Selfridges & Co
400 Oxford Street
London W1A 1AB
Tel: 020 7629 1234
www.selfridges.com
This store has a great modern furniture
department.

Viaduct Furniture
1–10 Summers Street
London EC1R 5BD
Tel: 020 7278 8456
An excellent selection of acclaimed
modern furniture designers.

Vitra Ltd
30 Clerkenwell Road
London EC1M 5PG
Tel: 020 7608 6200
www.vitra.com
This shop is particularly strong on
modern chairs.

modern rugs

Christopher Farr
212 Westbourne Grove
London W11 2RH
Tel: 020 7792 5761
www.christopherfarr.co.uk
Christopher Farr has a great selection of
colourful, modern handmade rugs, many
in geometric or abstract patterns.

Mosaik
10 Kensington Square
London W8 5EP
Tel: 020 7795 6253
www.mosaik-mesguich.com
Stocks a fantastic range of coloured or
patterned tiles.

Christine Van Der Hurd
Chelsea Harbour Design Centre
2–17 Chelsea Harbour
London SW10 OXE
Tel: 020 7351 6332
Hand-tufted bespoke carpets and rugs in
modern designs.

other exhibitions

The British Art Show
Tel: 020 7921 0837 for information.

Contemporary Art Society
17 Bloomsbury Square
London WC1A 2NG
Tel: 020 7831 7311
www.contemporaryorg.uk
Holds an art market of about 1,000 works
each autumn, most of them under £3,000.
A membership organization for collectors
or those interested in contemporary art.

Royal Academy of Arts
Burlington House
London W1V 0DS
Tel: 020 7300 8000
More than 1,000 works on display at the
annual summer exhibition, from amateurs
to RAs. Prices range from £50 for a print
to £70,000 for large sculptures.

picture framers

Colin Lacy
The Lacy Gallery
203 Westbourne Grove
London W11 2SB
Tel: 020 7229 6340
The doyen of antique frame dealers.

Paul Mitchell
99 New Bond Street
London W1Y 9LF
Tel: 020 7493 8732
Stocks more than 3,000 antique frames
and specializes in old and modern
masters. Cost for prints and drawings
£300–£3,000; paintings £3,000–£15,000.

FA Pollack
Unit 3, Rosebery House
70 Rosebery Avenue
London EC1R 4RR
Tel: 020 7837 6161

Rollo Whately
9 Old Bond Street
London W1X 3TA
Tel: 020 7629 7861

shops

uk

Egg
36 Kinnerton Street
London SW1X 8ES
Tel: 020 7235 9315
Stocks simple accessories and *objets d'art*
with an ethnic feel. Strong on ceramics.

Graham & Green
4–7 & 10 Elgin Crescent
London W11 2JA
Tel: 020 7727 4594
www.graham&green.co.uk
A great source of home accessories,
sourced from around the world.

Space
214 Westbourne Grove
London W11 2RH
Tel: 020 7229 6533
www.space@spaceshop.co.uk
Modern ceramics and other pieces.

usa

Totem
71 Franklin Street
New York 10013
Tel: (1) 212 925 5506
Modern furniture, lighting and
accessories.

sourcing contemporary art

The annual degree shows of the leading
schools and colleges are a fantastic
source of new talent.

uk

Goldsmiths College
New Cross
London SE14 6NW
Tel: 020 7919 7171
www.goldsmith.ac.uk
Wild and way out, but on a par with the
RCA when it comes to new talent.

The Royal College of Art
Kensington Gore
London SW7 2EU
Tel: 020 7590 4444
www.rca.ac.uk
The best place to spot the Peter Blake
or David Hockney of the future.

usa

Parson's School of Design
2 West 13 Street
New York 10011
Tel: (1) 212 229 8910
www.parsons.edu

textiles

The Gallery of Antique Costumes
& Textiles
2 Church Street
London NW8 8ED
Tel: 020 7723 9981
www.gact.co.uk

Guinevere Antiques
574–80 King's Road
London SW6 2DY
Tel: 020 7736 2917
www.guinevere.co.uk

Carolyn Quartermaine's Design Studio
Tel/fax: 00 44 207 373 4492

wallpaper & wallpaints

uk

Cole & Son Wallpapers Ltd
10 Chelsea Harbour Design Centre
London SW10 OXE
Tel: 020 7376 4628
3,000 wallpapers, made from handprinted
wood blocks (by commission), plus a
small range of period paints.

Colefax & Fowler
110 Fulham Road
London SW3 6RL
Tel: 020 7244 7427
Traditional, chintz-style wallpapers.

Neisha Crossland
Tel: 020 7823 7755 for stockists.
Fantastic modern wallpaper designs.

Tracy Kendall
Tel: 020 8769 0618 for stockists.
Beautiful, painterly wallpapers.

Cath Kidston
8 Clarendon Cross
London W11 4AP
Tel: 020 7221 4000
Sales@cathkidston.co.uk
Chintzy floral wallpapers in pretty colours
with a modern spin.

John Oliver
33 Pembridge Road
London W11 3HG
Tel: 020 7221 6466
Small, but excellent range of colours;
also grass cloth and paper weaves.

Paint & Paper Library
3 Elystan Street
London SW3 3NT
Tel: 020 7823 7755
www.paintlibrary.co.uk
A good range of paints and wallpapers by
Neisha Crossland, David Oliver, etc.

Sanderson
Tel: 01895 201509 for stockists.
A huge range of contemporary and historic
papers (including William Morris designs).

Ottile Stevenson
Tel: 020 7739 7321 for stockists.
Artistic range of contemporary wallpapers.

Jocelyn Warner
19–20 Sunbury Workshops,
Swanfield Street
London E2 7LS
Tel: 020 7613 4773
Graphic and floral printed wallpapers.

usa

Fine Paints of Europe
PO Box 419, Woodstock
VT 05091
Tel: (1) 800 332 1556
Colours inspired by natural sources.

Ralph Lauren Paints
Tel: (1) 800 379 7656 for stockists.
A great selection of colours.

INDEX

ACKNOWLEDGEMENTS

quotation sources

p. 8 Shaw, George Bernard, *The Penguin International Thesaurus of Quotations*, London, Penguin, 1985
p. 11 Bayley, Stephen, quoted in 'Pork Pies, Perspex and E-mailing' by Nicole Swengley, the *London Evening Standard*, 4 January 2000
p. 14 Warhol, Andy, quoted in *Living With Art* by Holly Solomon and Alexandra Anderson, New York, Rizzoli Publications, 1988
p. 27 Campbell, Nina, quoted in 'Interior Tatler' by Gail Rolfe, *Tatler* magazine, April 2000
p. 43 Mitchell, Paul, quoted in 'Picture Framers' by Alice Whately, *Harpers & Queen*, February 2000
p. 47 Richard MacCormac, quoted in 'Bouncing Off The Walls' by Hettie Judah, the *London Evening Standard*, 14 March 2000
p. 63 Gordon Clark, Jane, quoted in 'Wall to Wall' by Fiona McCarthy, the *Mail on Sunday* (*You* magazine), 23 January 2000
p. 76 Quartermaine, Carolyn, quoted in *Carolyn Quartermaine Revealed* by Kate Constable, New York, Rizzoli Publications, 1997
p. 94 Schimmel, Herbert and Ruth, information sourced from *Living With Art*, as above
p. 101 Beam, Jacob, quoted in *Living With Art*, as above
p. 120 Hilton, Matthew, quoted in 'Chair Crazy' by Tim Lusher in the *London Evening Standard*, 22 February 2000

further reading

Andrews, Tim *Raku: A Review of Contemporary Work*, London, A & C Black Publishers Ltd., 1994

Baker, Fiona & Keith *Twentieth-Century Furniture*, London, Carlton, 2000

Constable, Kate *Carolyn Quartermaine Revealed*, New York, Rizzoli Publications, 1997

Dixon, Tom *Rethink*, London, Conran Octopus, 2000

Fiell, Charlotte & Peter *1000 Chairs*, Cologne, Taschen, 1997

Livingstone, Marco *David Hockney*, London, Thames & Hudson, 1987

de Moubray, Amicia & Black, David, *Carpets For The Home*, London, Laurence King Publishing, 2000

Osterwold, Tilman *Pop Art*, Cologne, Taschen, 1999

Read, Herbert (Consulting Editor) *The Thames & Hudson Dictionary of Art and Artists*, London, Thames & Hudson, 1994

Solomon, Holly & Anderson, Alexandra *Living With Art*, New York, Rizzoli, 1988

picture credits

The publishers would like to thank the following sources for their kind permission to reproduce the pictures in this book:

t: top, b: bottom, l: left, r: right, tl: top left, tr: top right, bl: bottom left, br: bottom right, bc: bottom centre, bcl: bottom centre left, bcr: bottom centre right.

Danielle Arnaud Contemporary Art. For further information, contact: 123 Kennington Road, London SE11 6SF (020 7735 8292), www.daniellearnaud.com
Marie-Noelle Falticska, untitled 1998, pigment on paper 22t
Marie-Noelle Falticska, untitled 1998, pigment on paper 22bl
Marc Hulson *Trees (Halloween)* 2000, oil on canvas 19tr
Marc Hulson *Lost, Halflight and Face* 2000, oil on canvas 99t
Marie-France & Patricia Martin *Apres Richter, nu descendant*, 1993–8, photograph 99b
Marie-France & Patricia Martin *Body* 1998, photograph 22bl
Susan Morris *Witness* 1999, photographed by Susan Ormerod 19br
Gerry Smith *Zurich* 1997, oil on board 22t
Graham Atkins-Hughes 66, 70, 71, 74, 101r, 110l, 113l, 125, 147l
Graham Atkins-Hughes IPC Syndication/ *Living etc* 144tr

Jan Baldwin, wallpaper designed by Neisha Crosland and available from The Paint Library. Image courtesy of The Paint Library 1, 64tr
Jan Baldwin/Narratives 9, 23t, 36, 120t, 130bl, 132
Jibby Beane. Art direction: Jibby Beane, photography: Jonathan Gosland. Jibby designed her shell-like Clerkenwell apartment in 1997. Further information at www.jibbybeane.com 32, 154
Simon Brown/The Interior Archives 38, 63br, 63tr, 105l, 109tl, 109bl, 109r, 138tr, 138bl, 148, 153
Nicolas Bruant/The Interior Archives 5, 77, 83r, 84bl, 88, 112, 127, 131b

Jennifer Cawley 94tl, 94tr, 128

Furniture by Emmebi, courtesy of Geoffrey Drayton. Further information at www.geoffrey-drayton.co.uk 133br

Rene Gonkel 16, 24, 26, 120b, 122, 124

Timothy Green-Fields Saunders 29, 53

Ken Hayden/The Interior Archives 20

Ikea, courtesy of Condor Public Relations 55bl, 68bl
Tim Imrie IPC Syndication/*Family Circle* 78
International Interiors/Paul Ryan 15, 35, 57, 95

Deborah Jaffe 79l, 79tr, 100, 139b

Cath Kidston/*Vintage Style*/Ebury Press/Pia Tryde 80r, 89bl

Lalique, courtesy of Halpern Associates 151
Tom Leighton IPC Syndication/*Living etc* 79br

Ray Main/Mainstream 17, 23, 34, 43, 52br, 55t, 60br, 73l, 96tr, 101l, 102, 103, 110tr, 113tr, 113br, 114bl, 118, 126, 145, 136
Ray Main/Mainstream/Babylon Design 10
Ray Main/Mainstream/Architect Gregory Philips 40
Ray Main/Mainstream/Artist James Hugenon 46tl, 46tr, 47tl
Ray Main/Mainstream/Designer Vincent Wolfe 51
Ray Main/Mainstream/Designer Drew Plunkett 56
Ray Main/Mainstream/Artist Liz Ogilvie 86bl
Ray Main/Mainstream/Artist Henrietta Burnett 111
Ray Main/Mainstream/Usick/Heal 121
Ray Main/Mainstream/Designer Andrew Martin 123t, 134b
Ray Main/Mainstream/Architect Nico Rensch 134c
Ray Main/Mainstream/Designer Michael Sodeaux 135, 142
Ray Main/Mainstream/Designer Claire Nash 144br
Ray Main/Mainstream/Designer Sophie Chandler 147r
James Mitchell, represented by Penny Tattersall 18, 30, 31, 49, 90, 96b, 98tl, 115, 116
Eric Moran 60tr, 76, 85, 129, 131t
La Murrina 149tr, 149br, 150l, 150tr, 150br

Nick Pope IPC Syndication/*Living etc* 61, 64

Bill Reavell IPC Syndication/*Living etc* 58bl

Anna Silverton ceramics. Detail of cream stoneware vases. For further information, please contact 020 7358 9941 2–3, 140, 141
Howard Sooley 65
Rupert Spira 143t, 143b
Thomas Stewart IPC Syndication/*Living etc* 130tl

Tate Picture Library 133bl
Chris Tubbs IPC Syndication/*Living etc* 106
Sian Tucker 80l

Christine Van der Hurd 68tr, 68br, 69, 81
Verne 12, 72, 73r
Verne/Carlton Arms Hotel New York 59tr
Verne/Architect: Claire Bataille & Paul Ibens 52tl, 155
Verne/Architect: Boxy 62bl, 134t
Verne/Architect: Buro 2 54
Verne/Architect: Charles Cowles 44, 45
Verne/Architect: L. Gelfman 123br
Verne/Architect: Politi 25
Verne/Architect: Pruit & Early 28, 58br, 59br, 93
Verne/Architect: Glen Sestig 21
Verne/Architect: Hunt Slonem 97
Verne/Architect: Marina Spadalora 87
Verne/Architect: Vincent Van Duysen 62br

Daniel Ward IPC Syndication/*Living etc* 50, 75, 89tl, 108
Luke White 6, 41, 47, 48, 82, 86tl, 104, 105r, 133tr, 139t, 146
Luke White, location: Isabella and Detmar Blow's Home. Many thanks to Detmar and his gallery, Modern Art Inc 42, 107l, 107r, 119, 152
Polly Wreford IPC Syndication/*Living etc* 64br, 84br

YSL Mondrian dress, courtesy of YSL Press Office 83

Special thanks to: Luke White, James Mitchell, represented by Penny Tattersall, and Verne.

At the time of going to press, every effort has been made to acknowledge correctly and contact the source and/or copyright holder of each quotation and picture, and Carlton Books Limited apologizes for any unintentional errors or omissions which will be corrected in future editions of this book.

author's acknowledgements

I'd like to say a huge thank you to my agent Ali Gunn and to my commissioning editor Venetia Penfold and the rest of the hardworking team at Carlton Books, particularly project editor Zia Mattocks, art director Penny Stock, picture researcher Abi Dillon and copy editor Sarah Sears.

Special thanks to the following people for allowing their homes to be included in *Living With Art*: Danielle Arnaud, Jibby Beane, Isabella and Detmar Blow, Stella Blunt, Nick Ferrand, Lulu Guinness and Carolyn Quartermaine. Thanks also for their help to Linda Copperfield of the Saatchi Gallery, Jonathan Gosland (for photographs of Jibby Beane's self-designed apartment in Clerkenwell), Rupert Spira and Anna Silverton. Finally, big kisses to E and my mother and father for always being so enthusiastic.